A Time to
Embrace

awe

A Wife of Excellence
Life Study

Sandra Joan Goforth

This book is dedicated to all the women whose stories fill these pages. You have each given me a priceless gift — the treasures of your heart — and I pray God will use them to help countless women fall in love again.

Table of Contents

Chapter 6 ~ A Time to Choose Your Hormone

Chapter 7 ~ A Time to Help Your Man

Chapter 8 ~ A Time to Light the Fire

Chapter 9 ~ A Time to Negotiate

Chapter 10 ~ A Time to Practice, Practice, Practice

Chapter 11 ~ A Time to Cherish

Appendix

1

A Time to Talk About It

The Wedding Rehearsal Dinner

*T*hat night held no real historic significance, except I remember how I felt about him as we took our seats in the restaurant. He looked good – slate-gray hair freshly trimmed. Tonight, the smell of his cologne trumped the food, centerpiece flowers, and perfumed women crowding around us. I felt that delicious sensation of wanting the evening to end so we could get back home…

After it did end at the "pumpkin hour" for my age group, a-bit-after-ten, I felt as much exhaustion as romantic exhilaration. So when the cell phone buzzed at my feet, I almost didn't answer. *Really? At this hour – and not even out of the parking lot?* But I did pick it up, for a mom always answers her son's calls. His laugh on the other end deftly plopped a cherry on the ice cream sundae of the evening.

"Wow, Mom, I'm proud of you. Way to go tonight!"

"Thanks, son. It did feel good – and certainly not typical of me."

Right. My entire life I avoided argument at all costs – outside my immediate family, that is. If forced to engage in some conflict, any clever rebuttal came to mind long after the fact. But I'm getting ahead of the story.

The restaurant event room, elegantly bedecked with brightly-painted urns, flowers, and greenery cramped a U-shaped table arrangement for a hundred or so wedding participants and out-of-town guests. To us, this was an intimate gathering, for we knew so many of the participants. With one side of the U reserved for the wedding party, teen guests took up a section at the back, and the bride and groom sat at a table beside the speaker stand.

After a lively meal and raucous quiz game, the father of the groom invited guests to come forward and share congratulatory remarks or advice. Tentatively at first, one by one, well-wishers took the floor. One man encouraged the couple to be kind to each other in a fight. Another spoke of the need to readily forgive.

When the Best Man came forward with an impish grin, I thought surely now we'd receive the "toast" of the evening. The room quieted. Before speaking, he ceremoniously reached forward, picked up a salt shaker from the bride and groom's table, and held it high.

"They say (*cough, cough*) that newlyweds are, uh, quite active in the 'affection depart-ment' for the first year of marriage. Now, I know there are young ears present tonight so I will try to be, *ahem*, discreet..."

"Uh, yes, please do!" quipped a young father, hands cupped over his young son's ears. Guests chuckled and shifted in their seats. The bride and groom averted their eyes from anything in particular, as if hoping the earth would swallow them.

The groomsman cleared his throat and continued, "Well, they say if a couple puts a quart jar under their bed and deposits a penny every time they... you know... the idea is that, well, they'd fill that jar in the first year. Now, I am here to tell you the facts. This (*holding the shaker higher*) is all they'll need for their second year – hahaha! – and probably, hahaha, for the rest of their lives!"

He took his seat surely thinking his "blessing" a truly funny joke, but the audience didn't laugh. Though a few teens attempted an awkward chortle, we all sat in a sort of stupor.

Heavy is the best word I can think of. The air felt heavy. Someone else finally stood to speak, almost bringing levity back to the room, but my chest pounded as if it would burst. *Doesn't marriage deserve better? What about all the teenagers in the room looking for a future of great love and sex? They simply cannot think the best times are either behind them in the back seat of cars or ahead of them during a few months of honeymoon!*

After the next person finished speaking, I bolted from my seat. *Better not think about this. Just do it.* My mind reeled, but as I sprinted forward, a plan formed. Behind the bride and groom, urns of different sizes decorated a table. I picked up the largest one – about three feet tall – and, with no idea how fragile or valuable it might be, sort of stumbled to their table.

Passion must have run ahead of my fear for I heard words coming from my mouth. "Listen, you two. See this urn?" With my free arm I grabbed the salt shaker. "You will need a container closer in size to *this* (*nodding at the urn*) than *this* (*waving the saltshaker*) for your lifetime of pennies!"

At that moment, through the buzz of loud comments and giggles, someone raised his voice above the crowd. "That's my girl!" The room erupted in laughter. Yup. My hubby…

I somehow continued, "Marriage for us has been better than average. Not perfect of course, but lovely, because even after many years, we refuse to be a 'salt-shaker' kind of couple! We are determined to be an 'urn' couple. You can be, too."

Amid the applause, I gingerly set the urn back in place and returned to my seat. Throughout the rest of the night, one thought kept going through my head. *Marriage is worth fighting for! I must fight.*

Many years later, a friend purchased an urn for us to commemorate the wedding rehearsal dinner. Now it holds a place of honor in our bedroom. We don't put money into it but see it as a reminder to make love a priority. Our grown children and grand-children need our love to be strong. But most of all, we need our love to be strong.

1. $\mathcal{L}$ook back to a time you were out with your man when he looked very, very good to you. Tell about the scene and how the evening played out. ____

_____

_____

_____

2. $\mathcal{W}$hen did you speak up for marriage? How did it make you feel? What marital issue would you like to take a more public stand for? _____

_____

_____

_____

When you got married, did you feel the glow would wear off, or did you think your love would be different — that it would last forever? If you felt it would last forever, you got off on the right foot! Are you still on that sure footing or have you faltered?

5

Hopefuls in a World of Naysayers

Naysayers

Animated laughter filled the otherwise empty dining hall as about ten women engaged in disjointed babble around a circular table. By the time I pulled up a chair and squeezed in, they were already deep into some pretty tender topics – the day of their first period, their engagement, how much their moms told them about sex. Isn't that what usually happens when women gather? Not really. In this day and age, women find it hard to enter such discussions without kids walking into the room or a waiter coming up to the booth to ask to fill your glasses. Women wonder if others experience struggles in the long-term marriage as they do.

For quite a few years, a fire had burned in my soul to provide a place, a context for this kind of sharing, and that day, something clicked. I knew the time had come to go for it. A few friends from the group which had met serendipitously around the table helped me distribute a survey asking women over forty-five what issues most tripped them up in this season of life. Reading the results broke our hearts. We saw sexuality take the shape of boredom, resentment, and avoidance. Pain, scrawled in brief phrases on each page, revealed similar issues. "I can hardly stand to be touched sexually." "I feel so unlovely, how can he want me?" "I wish I liked my husband more."

Armed with the surveys and prayer, we approached our church to begin a small group for women in this stage of marriage. Without hesitation, they gave the All Go for our venture to launch. We called it AWE – A Wife of Excellence – with the stated purpose **to revive marital intimacy through a warm sexual relationship**.

The class began to gain momentum. Some came out of curiosity. *What? Are we really talking about this in church?* But most longed for a place where they could open up about marital issues that confused them. They wondered if they were alone. They hoped for answers. After promoting the class, *naysayers* could be heard in the church foyer. "This class may be fine for younger gals, but we had our day a long time ago – it's o-o-ver now."

Our first major test of confidence came when a pretty, fifty-something *naysayer* I'll call Debra showed up at a new AWE session. Before class even started, she proceeded to inform us our entire premise was wrong. "Listen, y'all. When we reach a certain age, we need to accept facts. Hormones are gone, and that signals the end of sex. Why fight the inevitable? You can't put pressure on women who are just glad to have the whole thing over! At this age, sex just isn't needed anymore." After class we thanked her for her perspective and for taking time to come. Though a bit shocked, I felt so relieved when the other women who came to test the waters returned the following week!

While driving home, I thanked God for Debra's visit and asked him to help me process her words. I wondered how many other wives think and feel as she does.. *and her comment about putting pressure on women… could our teaching somehow further hurt wives who carry deep wounds?* Debra didn't seem to fit that group; her only comment about her husband referred to his odd behavior of admiring his physique in the mirror after a shower. No, she definitely landed within the purview of our study. Still, I wanted clearer direction to move ahead.

I reviewed our purpose and revisited scriptures pertaining to sex, beginning with a deeper look at 1 Corinthians 7:1-5.

The husband should give to his wife her conjugal rights, and likewise the wife to her husband. For the wife does not have authority over her own body, but the husband does. Likewise the husband does not have authority over his own body, but the wife does. Do not deprive one another, except perhaps by agreement for a limited time, that you may devote yourselves to prayer; but then come together again, so that Satan may not tempt you because of your lack of self-control.

Though God tells us *to abstain only for short periods of prayer*, do these verses imply a hidden age limit for marital sex? Unless "do not deprive" refers to the *desire* of either partner, I couldn't find one. The phrase could mean that until *both* of you stops desiring sex, keep at it. But "do not deprive" seemed to me a challenge not to deprive *the marriage (each other)* of sexual involvement. If a convenient loophole opens for couples who *never deprive each other* because neither one asks the other for sex, they would seem to be in danger of falling into temptation. As for temptation, are we ever too old to be tempted sexually? Historically, categorically, no.

But I saw sexual temptation as a too-narrow meaning of self-control.

God's warning in verse 5, "…come together again, so that Satan may not tempt you because of your lack of self-control" might mean that prolonged abstinence could give Satan a foothold to come between a couple, to prevent them from working on their marriage in general. For, don't we lack self-control when we refuse to forgive quickly? **Don't we lack self-control when we stop listening to each other's heart issues in meaningful conversation? Could there be a connection between sex and the whole spirit of the marriage, apart from desire?**

When God revealed the text in that light, I felt convicted. If I am lazy in this area of marital sexual intimacy, don't I invite trouble in other areas? *Isn't my lack of self-control shown by ongoing selfishness or neglect? Even if, especially if, my husband's respectful deference keeps him from asking for sex?* That's really convicting, given the positive results of warm sexual involvement – to the couple, the family, and consequently, the whole community.

I continued to find support for our thesis in Genesis 2:24. "Therefore a man shall leave his father and his mother and hold fast to his wife, and they shall become one flesh." Regarding a "one flesh" relationship, I saw again that marital sexuality symbolizes a *deeper knowing and being known* as in the Hebrew word *yada*. If so, would God's purpose for sex in marriage change just because we age? If sex is more about heart intimacy, that *yada*, couldn't sexual relating continue even when normal intercourse is no longer possible?

In the Genesis story of Sarah and Abraham, I further questioned God. *Father, you could have brought your child of promise during their normal childbearing years, yet you chose to make them wait for decades. Why? Did they engage sexually (at least sometimes) into old age just in order to get pregnant? Or is it possible their sexual relationship helped keep their spirits from collapsing during such a long wait? Why does the scripture make a point of telling us that after Sarah died, Abraham remarried and fathered more children?*

I'd never asked these questions before, nor had I heard any sermons about the love life of Sarah and Abraham. Mere logic says that if Sarah and Abraham didn't engage sexually, they would, in actual biology, block the promised child. But if they *worked* at the relationship into old age, however stumblingly, wouldn't even this bless the world? God told Abraham he would bless all families of the world through Sarah and him!

These scriptural supports looked ironclad, yet I asked God to confirm our premise. *Father, are the fifties, sixties, and seventies a time of slowing down sexually for most couples? If so, what does that mean? Is sexual reconnection only a dream? Or, with some education, encouragement, and biblical understanding, can women rev their engines again, longer than they had thought before?* I believed they could. I'd seen my own answers to sexual needs over the years, but, like Gideon of old, I needed more confirmation.

Hopefuls

Then one day, Connie came – *a reluctant hopeful.* She walked into our spacious meeting room wearing a blue cardigan and white slacks – tall and strikingly elegant in her sixties. Of the nine ladies gathered on plump-cushioned couches, few knew what they were getting into; but by the end of introductory remarks, the topic was clear: sex, of the married kind, as mid-life brings new challenges.

Within minutes, Connie began to cry. Pulling a tissue from her purse, she sniffled and dabbed her mascara as we tried to avert our eyes. She even left the room once. Finally, before closing prayer, to everyone's great relief, Connie spoke. "I just don't think I can do this." More composed now, resolute, she said, "I knew what this class was about… and I know I need it. But I have issues…" Her chin dropped as her voice cracked, "…we've been out of the lovemaking habit a long, long time. I – I just don't have any hope."

Instantly, gentle pleadings filled the room. "Wait, Connie, I want to get to know you." "Give this a try." "Please come back one more time."

At the coffee bar after class, eyes still swollen, she met me alone. "It's been over twelve years since we've made love. He's a wonderful husband – maybe too wonderful, to go on and on like this. But my pain with sex – besides his prostate cancer issues – well, we're out of commission. Yet I know our marriage could be better. I just feel sad and so hopeless after all this time…"

"Connie, you don't need much hope, just a little. It obviously takes more than sex to make a good marriage, for yours seems good. God is at work. You're here! Let me ask you, if there were a one percent chance of being able to engage again sexually, would you come back to learn more?" Hesitantly, she agreed.

That was Tuesday. I prayed for her constantly. Would she show up again? As I entered the building the following week, a few women gathered in the hallway. The atmosphere felt strangely electric and warm. Connie stood among them, face beaming.

After everyone found their seats, Connie eagerly took the floor. Drawing a deep breath, she jumped in. "Well, here goes… Wes was hunched over our taxes at the dining room table after lunch, and I wanted to take a nap. But the longer I lay on the bed, the less tired I felt. My mind began to wander in his direction. I laid there and thought about how attractive a man he is, and good, and loving. My heart and body filled with feelings I'd not experienced for a very long time. Finally, I couldn't stand it any longer. I got up and walked into the dining room. I don't know why, but for some reason, I flipped the light off. I guess that got his attention. When I went over and took his hand, he looked up at me in the dark and said, 'What are you doing?'"

Connie's face flushed in a colorful mix of embarrassment and joy. "I just told him to come with me. We went to our guest bedroom and I said, 'Honey, we're going to make out.' Ha! You'd think he'd won the lottery… he got right into it and so did I. I felt things. I felt a new connection – even though it wasn't regular sex yet. We began a new life…"

The women sat speechless for a few seconds, though it seemed longer. In that moment of palpable tenderness and surprise, we all felt a keen awareness of how much God cares about our sex lives!

Someone dubbed Connie "Class Valedictorian," and we set off on our eleven-week journey of discovering a better path for this season of marriage. She not only soaked up the lessons like a sponge, she encouraged those who struggled and joyfully opened her home for our end-of-class celebration.

Of course, only wives attend our "hen parties." But when I entered the house that day, I could hear Wes' voice in the kitchen. Though he intended to leave, he stood around and chatted with the ladies till each one arrived. You see, he planned a little speech for us.

As Wes began to speak, the same electricity filled the kitchen as when Connie told of her rekindled passion. We all felt it. "I want to thank you ladies for giving me back the love of my life. I had a lovely wife before, but now I have a passionate lover. How, how can I thank you? I am overwhelmed…" And he began to cry. What a moment! Connie cried tears of longing and God met her need. Now her husband cried tears of joy.

That day, I knew without a doubt that God wants to make hopefuls out of naysayers. What about you? Do you think Connie might not be a relatable example for you? Do you see her experience as a bizarre kind of revelation? True, most people don't have dramatic "aha" moments where they suddenly change. But, think about it. A tiny rudder directs a huge ship; a small attitude adjustment changes perspective, tipping the scales from negative to positive. Connie's jolt wasn't a flash-in-the-pan sort of happening. She realized her attitude of failure and hopelessness dug a deep pit, a mire of lies. When she opened herself to truth, she found a fresh new path – for life!

Seeing what God had done in Connie and Wes' marriage, I knew we were onto something big. What's the big truth to embrace? You can start over! If your marriage is bogged down in the mire of complacency, pick up Hope. Walk over to your man, grab his hand, and get on a new path. We're here to help.

Present day update on Connie: At the time of publication, Connie and Wes continue their "honeymoon." As both stare down the upcoming age of seventy, they feel confident this renewed emotional bond will last forever. "I am truly 'in love' with my husband. God worked a miracle!"

2

A Time To Face Reality

Sarah's Day in Court

1 Peter 3:6
"…as Sarah obeyed Abraham… And you are her children,
if you do good and do not fear anything that is frightening."

I wish my stomach would stop churning. Everything will be fine.

The courtroom gallery fills with observers, poised for the crack of the judge's gavel. Everyone anticipates a dramatic climax to this highly-publicized trial, Satan vs. Marriage, which presents two opposing lifestyles.

Satan is suing Marriage for damages to his World System which claims the right of all people to a life of free sex for as long as they want it. The outdated custom of marriage, he says, must go. In opening statements, he mixes venomous barbs with buttery-smooth rhetoric, saying sexual activity dies in marriage and is replaced by boredom and vicarious romance from the media.

My job as the attorney for Marriage is to prove that a long-term covenant (life-time promise) is the rightful and best place for sexual fulfillment. I hope to prove that married sex which continues past childbearing years leaves a lasting legacy for grown children and grandchildren.

One by one, Satan calls women to the stand. Faces etched with lines of bitterness, they tell of betrayal and cheating by their husbands. Divorced women come forward to state that sexual variety (ie. various partners) beats bedroom boredom. Younger adults testify they don't want a marriage "like Mom and Dad have." Tearful wives tell of decades in abusive marriages, living in fear that to leave might cause more violence. Men take the stand and tout pornography as much easier than emotional intimacy. "Besides," one husband states, "you can't make a woman happy."

Hmmmm… is Satan building his case around fear?! The supposed enjoyment of sexual freedom, albeit short-lived, looks like his secondary line of reasoning. Good! Precisely why I chose my star witness, Sarah.

As you picture this drama unfolding, do you wonder who sits on the judge's bench? Who fills the jury? *You* do, my friend. You will make the final decision. Watch and listen.

Inhaling a deep shaky breath, I approach the bench. Before calling Sarah (from the book of Genesis) to the stand, I explain to the court how God singled out this couple to change the world, that every family in the world would be blessed through them. God promised that their child would start a new nation.[1] (Genesis 12:2, Genesis 22:18)

I silently pray observers will see Abraham and Sarah's long-term marriage as an example of hope and patience for us all. I explain that whether the court can relate to any of the specifics of Sarah's journey as a wife or not doesn't matter. They must look at the bigger picture – her whole life shows that submission is not blind obedience.

I remind the court of all the trials Sarah endured – pressures and traumas which would have caused terror, not just fear, in the most courageous of us. (Note to reader: Use your Bible for documentation of all these experiences or refer to the end notes with excerpts from the scriptures listed.)

- An excruciating cross-country move in a tent-caravan with hundreds of people – traveling over arid desert terrain to a new culture with different languages.[2] (Genesis 11:27-12:20)

- The huge weight of running a household with hundreds of servants, thousands of heads of livestock, and innumerable possessions.[3] (Genesis 13:2)

- Pressure to deny her identity as Abraham's wife (twice), putting her at risk of sexual assault in a king's harem, in order to preserve her man's goodwill and safety.[4] (Genesis 12:10-19 and Genesis 20:1-18)

- Enduring daily taunts and shunning by a friend and household employee whom she had trusted and eventually had to fire.[5] (Genesis 16:1-6 and Genesis 21:10-12)

- The constant threat of losing her husband as he trained and led to battle his own army – to protect his land and close relatives.[6] (Genesis 14:11-16)

- Trying for over 30 years to conceive. Birthing, nursing, and raising a child at ninety years of age – still alive when he became a teenager.[7] (Genesis 18:9-15)

Now, I call my witness, Sarah.

Me: Sarah, tell us about your marriage to Abraham?

Sarah: We made a lot of mistakes. Well, I made a lot of mistakes. Like when I gave up trying to have a baby – in my sixties, no less – and asked Abraham to take my maid Hagar as a surrogate. Hagar did get pregnant, but her baby was *not* the child God had in mind! The baby would come from my body, he said, no matter how long the wait. My relationship to Hagar was terribly strained. She treated me like I was the employee, not her. Thankfully, though, Abraham showed me much deference and honor when he let me send Hagar and Ishmael away. I had to do it! I had to establish my rightful place in our home.

Me: Is there another experience you want to share with us?

Sarah: Well, many people blame just Abraham when our travels put us in some awkward, as well as downright dangerous situations. They don't realize I agreed to the *sister version* of our relationship because he was so afraid of losing everything we had, possibly even being killed in hostile territory. Terrible things happened in the households of those leaders while I was in their palaces. At times, I was tempted to be afraid and very angry at Abraham, to doubt his love. But God protected me in ways that couldn't be explained. It all worked out.

Me: Sarah, you became pregnant with Isaac at age ninety. How were you able to wait so long for a child without giving up hope?

Sarah: I can only guess. Possibly our waiting revealed to us that God has the final say about his promises, *even through our many failures*. When God told my husband our wait was finally over, I inwardly laughed. But I didn't think anyone saw, even God. But he did. He knew my heart and asked me, "Is anything too hard for the Lord?" What a question! He was about to prove that nothing is too hard for him.

Me: Some people think you laughed because of the word "pleasure" in the Scripture. That you would experience pleasure in sex at that age. But that's not the case?

Sarah: Oh, no, I laughed because I couldn't believe I'd actually experience the pleasure of nursing and cuddling a baby! Because, you see, we never gave up sex. We couldn't. No matter how old we were, we had to keep working on our love life as well as other aspects of our marriage. Our sexual relationship helped us get through all the trials, and it eventually produced the promised miracle baby!

What about you, Judge and Jury? Think about your hopes for your marriage. Sarah was no different than you or me, except for being gorgeous at 89 years of age. She wanted love, normalcy, and a family. What she got was difficulty, pain, and endless waiting.

1. *T*ell of a time you felt abandoned by God, found nothing worked out as you'd planned. _____

_____

_____

_____

God reminds us in Isaiah 55:8 and 9, "...*my thoughts are not your thoughts, neither are your ways my ways.... For as the heavens are higher than the earth, so are my ways higher than your ways and my thoughts than your thoughts.*"

Who would have thought of femaleness and maleness but God? His character and love are expressed in the qualities of both sexes. He created two exquisitely different people, Adam and Eve, "naked and unashamed."

In Genesis 2:24, God speaks of leaving parents and clinging (cleaving) to a spouse in a deep "knowing" kind of love. One flesh. Remember the Hebrew word for this deep kind of knowing? *Yada.* God designed this intimate "knowing" kind of love to flourish in the safety and commitment of an exclusive relationship – marriage. Sex and marriage thrive together. Adam and Eve and God formed a rapturous triangle of communion and joy similar to the sweet communion among the Trinity – Father, Son, and Holy Spirit. They walked and talked together in paradise.

2. *C*opy Genesis 2:24 in your favorite version as a reminder of God's brilliant idea. _____

_____

_____

But things went terribly wrong when Adam and Eve disobeyed God's one and only command not to eat the fruit of the Tree of Knowledge of Good and Evil. When they ate, they opened themselves up to Satan's immediate and utter mutiny of sexuality.[8] (Genesis 3:6, 7) Instantly, their DNA changed. Their supposed *enlightenment* ushered in death. And death to oneness. They found each other not only embarrassingly naked, but untrustworthy, petty, selfish, and defensive. The brilliant authors of *Couples of the Bible,* Robert and Bobbie Wolgemuth, dramatizes the tragic event through the eyes of Adam.[9]

His night had been restless even after making love to his wife. The experience had been selfish rather than spontaneous and joyful, coerced instead of rollicking. It was not good.

Trying to push back pangs of the guilt of his fruit-eating disobedience, Adam tried to talk with God, his Friend. But his words were hollow and awkward. God, who had once felt so close, suddenly felt far away.

Adam groaned audibly. He knew that what they had done in the garden had destroyed his perfect companionship with Eve. His relationship with his wife was now laced with mis-understanding and heartache. And strain. Just that morning he had spoken thoughtless and searing words....

Sound familiar? Thankfully, God provided a merciful way out of the mess they *passed on to us.* He loved mankind so much that he came to earth and willingly died to pay the penalty we owed, bridging the huge chasm between us and his perfection. Jesus Christ died to gain a personal relationship with us[10] (John 3:16)! Christ's violent death on a cross proves what deep down we all know – suffering truly is the currency of love.

The following pyramid shows four purposes for sex.

Procreation

P L E A S U R E

Oneness Between Husband and Wife

A Picture of Christ's Love for Us, His Bride

Though the church has traditionally embraced **procreation** as the most important purpose for sex – and **pleasure** as second – it has not properly acknowledged the deeper purposes for sexuality which we believe make all the difference in both our relationship to God and to our mate. However, most people in our culture view pleasure as the most important, though shaky and elusive, purpose of sex. Always on the search for a better high, we find ourselves in a maze of insecurity while we hunt for more pleasure.

Speaking of elusive, the third level of our pyramid – **emotional oneness** – is only a distant dream for many, if not most. They see it in the movies and in novels. They sometimes *think* they see it in social media. But, having a couple of children and a bit of fun while relatively young, they think that's the best they can get. For

sooner or later, won't the pleasure run out? Have you noticed the average length of a Hollywood relationship? About three months if it's a "serious" one.

The main purpose for sex, **a picture or metaphor of Christ's love for us, his Bride,** reveals the depth of commitment in marriage as it is meant to be. To understand it we have to know we are loved by a God whose love endures forever.[11] (Jeremiah 31:3) The Bible has been called God's *love letter* to us.

3. Read a few of the hundreds of Bible passages professing God's love for us: John 3:16, Psalm 36:7, Psalm 86:5, and Romans 5:8.[12] Choose which verse most personally speaks to *you*. Copy it here. _____

_____

_____

_____

_____

God loves us, the church, so much he calls us his bride. He also called the Israelites of the Old Testament his bride. Why? It has everything to do with the bigness of his love. It is so big we can't grasp it. To help us get an earthly picture of something out of our realm of understanding, he made sex. Our desire for sex is meant to drive us toward the lover of our souls!

In Ephesians 5:28-33, Paul compares our marital union to that of Christ and us, the church.

> *In the same way husbands should love their wives as their own bodies. He who loves his wife loves himself. For no one ever hated his own flesh, but nourishes and cherishes it, just as Christ does the church, because we are members of his body. Therefore a man shall leave his father and mother and hold fast to his wife, and the two shall become one flesh. This mystery is profound, and I am saying that it refers to Christ and the church. However, let each one of you love his wife as himself, and let the wife see that she respects her husband.*

A wedding ceremony includes a set of vows or promises two people make to each other. When a couple writes their own vows, they throw in words like "forever" and "always." We really have no idea what we're saying, for these words usually mean "as long as you make me happy." But God's love for us is a covenant, a truly forever kind of love. Marriage is meant to be a picture of that.

A married couple mysteriously and joyfully acts out this deep *knowing* in the sexual joining of their bodies. Each time they make love, they, in essence, renew their *covenant* promise to each other. What an amazing thought!

Now, can you see why I chose Sarah for my star witness? Love isn't a mushy, gushy emotion. It's gritty and difficult, fraught with testings and trials. To get through, we need to know we are loved by a faithful God, cherished amid all manner of confusion. And if sex is inextricably tied to the marriage relationship in its fundamental purpose, we must endure some suffering and learn what this part of the equation looks like.

As you answer these questions, ask God to open your heart to believe, really believe, he loves you. That's the starting point of seeing your marriage differently.

4. Most of us have "something" related to our marriage we've desperately wanted for years. We've wanted something to either stop happening or something to happen. But it hasn't stopped or happened yet – or we haven't received it. What have you been waiting for? How does Sarah's wait encourage you?

_____
_____
_____
_____
_____
_____

Our opening verse from I Peter 3:6 tells us we are Sarah's daughters if we "do good and do not fear anything that is frightening." In her marriage, Sarah was not a doormat. Juli Slattery tells us in her book, *Finding the Hero in Your Husband*, "Sarah... clearly played an active role... She respected Abraham and gave him final authority to make decisions, but she did not withhold her feelings and opinions..." We know that on several occasions Abraham listened to her and God went so far as to tell him to do what she said.[13]

5. $\mathcal{N}$ame at least one fear you have now or have had in your relationship. How does Sarah's refusal to fear, even while enduring so much pain, inspire or encourage you today?_____

_____

_____

_____

_____

As the judge in this courtroom, you decide who wins. Satan's and the world's thoughts about love and marriage? Or God's views on the subject? Ask God to take away your fear about the future. He can and will fulfill your hopes in his timing, in his way, and on his terms. But he is always good, always faithful regarding his beloved – you.

$\mathcal{W}$rite a prayer expressing your desire to hang in with the desires you have for your marriage._____

_____

_____

_____

_____

_____

_____

_____

War of the Microphone

The battle over sexuality rages between progressive modernism, an evolutionary worldview, and Christianity, a worldview based on the Bible. The church is caught in the crossfire. No matter how loud or enthusiastic our worship music, the culture perches on its media soapbox and preaches with the most effectiveness. Meanwhile, the church, in its desire to stay relevant, remains silent. In a world where moral absolutes are shunned, the world's morality stands on its own two absolutes: what I want and when I want it. Notice how the culture war affects marriage at every age and season.

Evolutionary Worldview	Christian Worldview
Sex is a normal part of dating, courting.	Sex symbolizes commitment, belonging.
Sex is a physical need, like food.	Sex is a physical/emotional desire, not need.
Man is incomplete without sex.	Man is incomplete without God.
Naughty is nice. Do what feels good.	Sex under God's authority *is* pure and good.
Man is a product of genes and instinct.	Man's will and heart win over instinct.
Family is who you say it is.	Family is parents and children (incl. adoption).
Divorce is natural if things go sour.	Disposing of marriage hurts all involved.

Open Marriage can work and is not abnormal.	Marriage is meant to provide security in fidelity.
Sexual interest determines sexual identity.	We are born with gender – male and female.
Sexual Identity is fluid, can change.	We can't control gender.

The Modern Church
Teaches that God understands our weaknesses and overlooks them.
Promotes compassion for sexual *behavior*, not just the "*sinner.*"
Believes the Bible can be interpreted to allow for personal identity.
Prefers silence on some scriptures than risk being thought "out of touch."
Maintains that *experts* are better equipped than parents to teach sexuality.
Touts Christ's warning not to judge or throw stones unless we are without sin.
Asks: Who are we to determine hard rules when Christ did away with the law?

Dear Father,

Forgive us for standing by and allowing the sexualization of our society through the blaring microphone of the media. We see the carnage all around us – broken lives and shattered dreams of fulfilling love and joy in a secure marriage. Help us turn to your words and your ways for you are the one who created real, lasting sexuality. Help us learn to be examples our children and grandchildren want to follow – humble, kind, and available to our imperfect mates – thus reclaiming the microphone for this generation.

In Jesus' Name, Amen

Sexually Stuck Women

Remember Debra, our vocal naysayer? Like many women in their early fifties, she honestly thought life would be fine now without sex. Other women, like Connie, suffer emotional pain well into their sixties because they long for a closer relationship and don't know how to get it. Connie hungered for a marriage like her daughter's, whose husband bought her a massage table for Christmas. The gift included a weekly massage for the entire year. Though Connie loved her husband, she couldn't seem to bridge the gap from the friendship of doing life together to a passionate connection in the bedroom. Her mental tapes played on a constant loop. "I can't," "It hurts," "It's been too long…"

More wives than you would imagine secretly live in shutdown mode. I heard of an older evangelist who sometimes opened conversations with couples by asking,

"When did your biggest marriage problem start?" When a couple would reply, "How did you know we have issues?" he would say, "Well, you're married, aren't you?"

Symptoms of the Sexually Stuck Woman

The most common symptom of being sexually stuck is simply not having regular, pleasant sex when sex is available, i.e. you're married! The following list, however, helps narrow down behaviors and feelings cited for shutdown. Mark each one which applies to you. Circle the one which gives you the most trouble.

_____ 1. Sex hurts.

_____ 2. I am no longer interested, and he never mentions it.

_____ 3. I'm too busy and never even think about sex.

_____ 4. I wish I still had interest, but with younger kids in the house, I can't go there.

_____ 5. I'm always too tired.

_____ 6. I feel old – unlovely, overweight, or wrinkled.

_____ 7. I am too angry with him to engage.

_____ 8. I am interested but he rarely or never wants me.

_____ 9. He's always after me for sex – I feel like a sex object.

_____ 10. He doesn't compliment/respect me, so I feel cold.

_____ 11. Sex is boring – same time, same way, same everything.

_____ 12. His comments, i.e. sexual jokes and innuendo, annoy/disgust me.

_____ 13. With so much on my mind, even though I'd like to, I can't "focus" during sex.

_____ 14. He can't "perform" sexually and has given up on it.

Causes of Wives' Shutdown

By examining how we got stuck in the first place, we can decide how to move toward a better relationship. As you read the most commonly reported causes of shutdown and respond to the questions, don't be alarmed if several match your situation. Instead, be encouraged! In the pages ahead, we will address them in more detail.

Physical Change

It's impossible to over-emphasize the effect hormones and aging have on a woman's sexual interest. One day we're sweet and lovey-dovey, the next we're like the wife from the netherworld. As a matter of fact, Chapter 5 is devoted to the troubles which arise from these fluctuations.

Journaling helped me as I experienced severe PMS during my thirties and forties. I recorded libido ups and downs on a calendar set aside for just that purpose. I rated myself each day on a scale of 1 to 5 with 5 meaning "Very Interested" and 1 meaning "No Interest." This information helped me give myself a break and not see "us" as the problem on the days sex had no lustre.

Though libido is a fickle friend even in the best of worlds, when menopause enters the scene, hormones can seem to launch an all-out attack on desire. Women report:

a. After my hormones died down, his advances seemed more annoying.
b. I hate my body now — sagging breasts, weight gain, wrinkles, arthritis — definitely not sexy.
c. Lower energy, no libido… with a busy life, I never think about sex — ever.
d. If Hubby's sex drive takes a dive as well as mine, well, I say "Forget it."

1. Which of these thoughts do you relate to? When did these thoughts set in? How have they changed your love life? What other thoughts about hormonal changes have blocked you? _____

_____

_____

_____

_____

A Different Kind of Busy

On the radio program, *Focus on the Family*, Dr. James Dobson used to say, "If you are too busy for sex, you are too busy." We can readily add, "If you are too tired

for sex, you are too tired." Yet women cite the tired problem more now than ever. Recently, interviews with couples of all ages have shown that fewer than 30% make love as often as once a week. The most common reason for not hitting that mark is reported as busyness. In the old days, if libido fought for attention, it often won. Back then, busy was the "have to" kind, like cleaning house, cooking, going to work, bathing children.

What about now? Do teenagers run you ragged with various events? And if the kids are gone, they are never completely gone. Their adult lives pull you in a thousand ways, often to different cities. It's a complicated juggling act. You join a Bible study, you volunteer, you teach a Sunday class. Dip, lunge, catch, throw - always in a hurry. You've added a "want to" kind of busy which affects your already lower libido. At night, all you can think of is... sleep.

2. *W*hat kind of busy has interrupted your priority of a sexual encounter?

_____

_____

_____

The Rift – Built-Up Resentments

Issues from both families of origin often surface right around the quarter-century mark when we're launching our kids. Misunderstandings, which used to be like a 90-pound weakling, grow to bully-sized dimensions, plowing resentments into the relationship. Differences you once thought would "just go away" don't. Fights get harder to resolve. Sometimes low libido in either husband or wife tends to put off the needed conversation, the needed forgiveness. In quiet moments you work it all around in your head. *I know I have to forgive him in order to make love to him – but again!? No, it's just too hard. He does the same thing over and over again...*

While years roll by, rifts dig a pit, whether cyclical or erratic. Maybe a particular season of the year triggers pain and avoidance. Maybe conflict doesn't pay off because your marriage dynamic has deteriorated over the years. Fights escalate instead of resolve. Like the slow onset of death in a running car parked in a closed garage, romance silently suffocates and dies under the weight of accumulated, unresolved "stuff." *Sex? I can't even think about it*

3. *W*hat recurring fights, only slightly buried, threaten your love life?____

_____

_____

_____

The Drift

Kissing and touching can easily fall by the wayside. Your spouse becomes a roommate or business partner. Even without daily conflict or built-up resentments, couples drift. Like two boats side by side in still water always drift apart unless tied together, we must be aware of each other. Those kisses that used to be a natural part of the day made life much better than we realized. We took them for granted, didn't we?

What do you think? Will happy couples gradually stop "Kitchen Kissing?" My money says they will – unless one (or both) keeps the practice going on purpose. Think of a time when going through the day without kisses and hugs seemed impossible.

4. *W*hen did fun, relaxed relating stop? Why do you think it stopped?____

_____

_____

_____

_____

No More Date Nights or Getaways

When you were dating, fun was a priority. Why not now? If fun isn't a priority anymore, weekend getaways probably fall farther down the To Do List, too. Does fun now revolve around the grandkids? Unless you push *alone time* to the forefront, almost anything can push it aside. Sex will probably fade away as well.

If you danced before, do you still dance? If you skied, do you still ski? If you hiked, is hiking over? When illness or injury forces an extended break, many couples move on to a new boring chapter of marriage. Getaway weekends just for talk, sleep, sex, and recreation are too important to let slide.

5. *W*hen was your last getaway?_____

_____

_____

6. *W*here did you go?_____

_____

_____

7. *H*ow do you remember it? (pictures, souvenirs for family and hubby to see)

_____

_____

_____

8. *W*hat local activities have you enjoyed together lately? How did you make them a memory? _____

_____

_____

_____

_____

As you thought about these questions, could you see the sinister enemy, Romantic Laziness, thwart the original attention and tenderness you and your husband fostered through careful care? Why do we sabotage ourselves by doing what's easy, rather than what's best? Our selfish human nature procrastinates. *I'll weed the garden tomorrow.* Yet, it's crazy… we will sometimes choose to weed vegetables in the unbearably hot sun than spend quality time working on our most valuable asset – our marriage.

When Sex is All About Him

Let's look at three common ways sex can be all about him. Sometimes you've encouraged the situation, inadvertently letting your libido die. If his behavior is the problem, have you allowed it?

a. A husband goes to bed a few hours after his wife and decides to wake her up for sex. This practice makes sex the easy, semi-conscious *man-fix*. Wives everywhere have been known to say, "Fine. Just don't wake me up completely."

b. In the Dimestore Quickie, men initiate sex and finish in only a few minutes. This was never God's design. Sadly, women get stuck thinking this is normal sex. A necessary "gift" for their husbands – a duty.

c. Other husbands who just want to be wanted would never think of the quickie as normal sex. But they sense they aren't desired so resort to quick sex. If he seems irritable or "off" with you a few hours or a day after sex, his attitude makes you feel less and less *benevolent*; he becomes less attractive to you. Sex is all about him by default because you aren't talking about it.

Do any of these scenarios seem familiar? Are you relieved if your hubby expects no pleasurable response from you? Are you resentful that sex seems all about him? You're in the right place. How good to know that whether men acknowledge it or not, they need and want their wives' help to be good lovers.

9. If you are sexually stuck because sex is all about him, write here which scenario describes your version and how you think it got started. _____

_____

_____

_____

_____

_____

Sexual Abuse from the Past

At least one in four women in the over-fifty age bracket has been sexually abused in her lifetime. When you consider women in every age group, the statics go up to about half. In just our AWE classes, where women are generally over forty, about half report past abuse.

Even when memories lie buried for many years, sexual abuse affects almost every area of a woman's life. In many ways, abuse renders her unable to feel autonomous. Women struggle, sometimes profoundly, with decision-making, confidence in self and others, motivation to excel, wholeness, and a vibrant sex life.

Professional counseling often provides the best path to emotional health. Also, the excellent book, *Wounded Heart* by Dan Allender, has transformed many broken lives. Both men and women have been healed through his groundbreaking work in this area. Don't give up. God has much in store for you as you read and stretch and see more each day how precious you are in his sight – as well as your husband's.

10. *W*ere you molested or sexually assaulted as a young girl or teenager? Did a relative taunt you with lewd remarks? Did your parents fail to protect you from someone in the community who took advantage of your innocence? Write briefly about it here._____

_____

_____

_____

_____

_____

The Husband Who is Seriously Stuck

What happens when your husband's desire hits empty? You no longer feel the pain of rejection. You're beyond talking. You're beyond seducing. You're even beyond counseling. You're both stuck.

Many and varied issues cause the over-fifty husband to shut down sexually. Whether young or old, a man's sexual difficulty, combined with his emotional reaction to it, makes the problem a serious one.

A question which comes up regularly in class goes something like this. "Where are the men's small groups on this topic?" Churches do need mentoring for men. The whole realm of sexuality, hijacked by our enemy, Satan, needs to be reclaimed for God's purposes. As we, the church, call out leaders for this vital ministry, the fact remains, you and I, dear sisters, are the ones here. We can effectively change the dynamic in our marriage.

Once we stop feeling helpless and decide to roll up our sleeves and learn what we can do to improve the situation, men can be encouraged and empowered to change as well.

In these pages, you will learn ways to practically help your mate be the man he wants to be.

11. If your husband is sexually stuck, how will you commit to help him?

_____

_____

_____

12. The above causes of shutdown may not apply to you. You may not be shut down or stuck at all. Write about your present state. Remember, prolonged illness, injury, past widowhood, a non-sexual trauma, or a husband's pornography addiction may lead to sexual shutdown. Use this opportunity to examine your unique situation._____

_____

_____

_____

_____

❧ ❧

Prayer

I need your help. Sometimes I feel like a failure as a lover because I don't want to have sex with my husband very often. I selfishly use my lack of libido or tiredness as an excuse. Please give me your perspective! Help me see my husband as worthy of every effort to relate to him sexually. I know all these tips would help us. Give me courage to try a few of these ideas. I know you will bless us for taking time for sex. Help me learn to enjoy him in a whole new way.

In Jesus' Name, Amen

❧ ❧

3

A Time to Start Moving Forward

Those Little Relational Things and What Happens When...

Ephesians 4:32
"Be kind to one another, tenderhearted, forgiving one another,
just as God in Christ Jesus has forgiven you."

On Memorial Day weekend, Ned noticed Jenny didn't return his squeeze of her hand during church. That Sunday night, when he clicked off the bedside lamp, she offered no usual lovey words or warm kiss in response to his.

Next morning, while making breakfast together in a silent kitchen, Ned knew today would be difficult for Jenny. Today, no mini-humans would tear into the house with quick hugs, anxious to play and later dig into hamburgers and watermelon; this year, the in-laws won the draw at the last minute. He knew what was going on with Jenny because they'd established a healthy sort of barometer over the years – "little things."

After topping off Jenny's coffee, Ned leaned across table, looked directly into her eyes, and stroked her arm. When she returned his gaze, he said, "Hey, let's go do something today."

Those little relational gestures not only make life sweeter, they impact our love life. Warm hugs and a "How are you doing?" aren't really little, are they? As years go by, they seem to take even more intentionality, yet when forgotten, may hasten the end of lovemaking. And when that happens, the dynamic in the home changes – for the worse.

In this section, you will take two separate, though somewhat connected surveys. First, your relationality (or is it relationicity?). Second, you will venture a guess as to what happens when lovemaking stops.

Some couples argue they have a great sex life with no need for the relational behaviors listed below. Those claims may arise out of the way a partner's family of origin did or didn't show affection. Some families never even think of these gestures. But these little things, a touch or kiss or consideration, influence our overall relationship.

Simply check the items below which you practice more or less regularly. If you don't touch often, notice the list contains both touch and non-touch behaviors. You can get a high score for a relational marriage either way.

Those Little Relational Things

_____ 1. A quick smile or eye contact while passing in the hallway or tight space.

_____ 2. Some friendly touch or pat in the kitchen while preparing food or eating.

_____ 3. A warm kiss when leaving the house for an errand, evening, or workday.

_____ 4. A smile and kiss of greeting when arriving home.

_____ 5. A goodnight kiss before falling asleep.

_____ 6. Touching/cuddling at least occasionally while sleeping.

_____ 7. Holding hands while walking, watching TV, driving in the car.

_____ 8. Light mealtime discussion.

_____ 9. A morning greeting when waking up.

_____ 10. Intentional eye contact while the other talks.

37

_____ 11. Calling or texting regularly just to say, "Hi, how are you?"

_____ 12. Cell phones moved to another room during meals or while talking.

_____ 13. Very limited use of cell while driving in car together.

_____ 14. *Not checking cell phone notifications till after a meal or talk.

_____ 15. *Willingly leaving an event when the other person gives you "the nod."

_____ 16. *Deferring to mate's wishes in a non-consequential issue you disagree about.

Notice the starred items? They give you two points instead of one. Why might these deserve extra credit? If you scored more than 8 points, you are a relational couple. If you found less than 5, it may be time to improve your *relationability*.

Score: _____

After finishing the book, take the survey again: *Second score*: _____

1. *L*ist three little things you will start working on today. We all need accountability to establish new routines or meet goals. Here's an idea to help you. Write your goals on a small card and put it in the personal (not shared) bedroom or bathroom drawer you open most often. Each time you open it, ask yourself if you worked on the behavior yesterday, and how you can work on it today. _____

_____

_____

One wife wanted to be more diligent about kissing her husband when leaving the house (for longer than half a day) and upon returning. She checkmarked her bathroom card after a successful week. After four checks, she rewarded herself to a spa splurge. The main reward, of course, was the change in their relationship. Things warmed up quite a bit because of her attention to this one "little thing."

What Happens When A Couple Stops Making Love

If the above gestures go by the wayside, sexual activity may soon follow. Researchers define as sexless the marriage which has sex less than ten times a year. Remember Connie from "Naysayers and Hopefuls?" After over twelve years with no sexual involvement, their relational marriage kept the door open for a renewed love affair. Though their story shows that a good relationship requires more than sex, counselors agree that married people rarely have a mutually satisfying relationship without the sexual component. Even if a couple believes they are "content" without sex, the following survey may help reveal the true level of contentment.

Based on observations of relationships close to you or a time in your own marriage, now or in the past, check the statements below which seem true. There are no right answers here. Take time to share your answers and give reasons.

_____ 1. One (or both) feels emotional distance in the relationship.
_____ 2. One or the other seems sad — less smiling, less laughing around the house.
_____ 3. Fighting increases (or worse, stops completely); issues are harder to resolve.
_____ 4. One or the other seems or even acts older.
_____ 5. New, fun activities are rare, and when they happen, are anticipated less.
_____ 6. Husband doesn't comment as much on his wife's underwear, clothing, jewelry.
_____ 7. Fewer hugs and kisses around the house.
_____ 8. Husband hardly notices when wife is naked.
_____ 9. Irritations, picking, and bickering are more common.
_____ 10. Neither one readily asks for forgiveness. Restoring tenderness is harder.
_____ 11. If apart for several days (or all day), they don't miss each other.

2. $\mathcal{M}$any underlying issues can cause the above problems in a marriage. All marriages are complicated. Whether you checked all or only a few of the items above, discuss how stopping sex may have started the negative dynamic in the home. Write your thoughts here as well as helpful thoughts from others in your group. _____

_____

_____

_____

_____

Prayer

Lord, help me to think carefully about the importance of these things. I want a warm, tender atmosphere in our home. Show me how I can begin to foster a more open and Christ-like attitude today?

In Jesus' Name, Amen

Which Gal Are You?

Romans 8:38
"For I am sure that neither death nor life, nor angels nor rulers,
nor things present nor things to come, nor powers, nor height nor depth,
nor anything else in all creation, will be able to separate us
from the love of God in Christ Jesus our Lord."

"My husband is frustrated with me, again! This keeps happening, and I keep thinking we're past it. I'm so frustrated with him for being frustrated with me!"

I had driven to the women's retreat angry and defensive. Now, clothes hung, suitcase stashed in the closet, my friend finally settled on her bed and exhaled a long sigh. "Sandi, don't be surprised at this — or your feelings about it. You need this marriage ministry as much as the rest of us. Ya gotta let it go, or see it his way."

So much for commiseration.

In bed that night, it hit me. Like Annie in the personas below, I felt compelled to react with indignation instead of humble vulnerability. I thought again how so many factors from my past affected how I naturally related to my husband. How in my teen

41

years, for some reason I began a pattern of stealing hearts and promptly breaking them. Why did I do that?

What about your adolescent and college years? Were you the serious fall-in-love-and-stay-with-one-guy type, or did you play the field? Parental influences, birth order /sibling issues, traumas in childhood or adolescence, and even our natural temperament all work together to develop self-protective behaviors long before marriage.

This distancing comes from hurt. No one escapes. While our experiences may not look the same, feelings of alienation from the love of God may cause us to develop coping skills which keep hurt as far away as possible. The result is even more brokenness and a greater sense of separation in relationship.

Today, let's look at personas we may have inadvertently adopted: Anxious Annie, Self-Righteous Sue, Diva Donna, and Bruised Barbara. As you read about each one, with whom do you identify the most?

Anxious Annie
Key Issue: Negativity

_____ **Annie is outwardly compliant in nature.** Her "good girl" persona earned her Mr. Almost Perfect, albeit a fleeting title. When she tried to tweak him, the honeymoon ended. A bright light in public, she can be downright petty, negative, fearful, and needy at home. In her self-protective mode she withholds affection in hopes her man will "step up" and make her happy. Of course he doesn't, so with perimenopause on the scene, her emotions going haywire, depression lurks around the corner.

Marital disconnect can sometimes turn the Annies of the world toward a more genuine relationship with God. We Annies must grow up, accept responsibility, become a giver not a taker, and drop unrealistic expectations. But how can we do it?

1. *W*hat will help Annie be less selfish and approach her husband again?

_____

_____

_____

2. $\mathcal{H}$ow might you be Annie?_____

_____

_____

_____

Self-Righteous Sue
Key Issue: Complacency

_____ **Sue, an overachiever, plows through obstacles.** Though her marriage may be a bit stale, she keeps herself under constant pressure to *seem* happy. Always busy serving, leading church and civic groups, she stays cool. She cleans and cooks up a storm, yet tends to withdraw from sexual intimacy. She figures if she doesn't expect much of him, he won't expect much of her. Too busy to cuddle or talk, the juggling balls of perfection are about to drop. Though her husband may be patient, his long-suffering may wear thin.

God can meet Sue in honesty and brokenness. His grace will help her join the frail, imperfect human race.

3. $\mathcal{H}$ow can Sue maintain her leadership skill and roles without neglecting her marriage? _____

_____

_____

_____

4. $\mathcal{H}$ow are you like Sue?_____

_____

_____

_____

Diva Donna
Key Issue: Manipulation

_____ **Donna must look lovely at all costs,** at all times – for somewhere along the way, she learned that beauty opens doors. While beauty is synonymous with femininity, Donna also finds joy in things and social activities. After marriage and pregnancy though, Donna became moody, withholding affection unless she got what she wanted to keep up her lifestyle. Through financial ups and downs, she often used sex as a trading chip. Also, aging made her feel unlovely. Donna never learned to love with abandon.

God can bring inner confidence, emotional openness, and help Donna let outer beauty fade as her inner beauty grows.

5. How can Donna see aging as beautiful, not dowdy? How can she experience emotional freedom? _____

_____

_____

_____

6. How might you be Donna? _____

_____

_____

_____

Bruised Barbara
Key Issue: Avoidance

_____ **Barbara carries the burden of an abusive and/or rebellious past.** Profound wounds almost always precede rebellion. She can't escape the pain of what happened back then and still feels shame. Even with an excellent education and lucrative career, every household chore takes too much effort. While sex may have been a normal part of her former party life, she shudders now when her husband approaches her. Where before she thought, "I must have sex," now her thoughts scream, "*Must* I have sex?!"

Christ came to heal every Barbara! He lifts the burdens we ask him to take off our back and removes the pain. He can help her know her sins are removed "as far as the east is from the west." Read Psalm 103 for a reminder of how God loves Barbara.

7. Copy your favorite verse from this Psalm. _____

_____

_____

_____

8. Now read Isaiah 54:3-9. How can God replace Barbara's ashes with a true, abiding love for her husband, as well as a sense of beauty and joy in aging?

_____

_____

_____

9. How might you be Barbara? _____

_____

_____

_____

Jillian

When Jillian learned about the personas, she discovered that at some time in her life **she'd lived in all four.** "I am a royal mess!" she said. As Annie, she assumed the "good girl" role during her teens – staying emotionally detached from boys, getting the best grades. Besides winning college Homecoming Queen (Donna), she pursued a brief stint in modeling. While raising two kids, the local school board asked for her help, and she worked tirelessly for several years (Sue).

Yet at age forty-four, when perimenopause symptoms began, she regained a lost memory of molestation as a child (Barbara) and sank into a sense of powerlessness.

A Time to Start Moving Forward

For the past ten years, depression threatened her marriage and parenting. If you saw her in the store or at church, you'd never know. Her amazing beauty belies the fact that heartache lives under her smooth surface.

Jillian rated each persona (1 to 5) for the effect it had on her attitudes in marriage:

- Barbara, 5, the most effect, because of insecurity which hounded her during recent menopausal years.
- Anxious Annie, 4, slightly less but still significant, because of fears which created her "good girl" identity as a youth.
- Donna, 4, for she struggles to accept her aging. Beauty consumes much of her time.
- Sue, 2, for the least effect, because her "outfront" jobs lasted a short time.

When Jillian evaluated her marriage in light of these personas, she realized her need for a new identity — one founded on what God says. By memorizing passages from Isaiah 54:1-8 and 55:12-13, as well as verses from Romans 8:31-39, she began to experience a new era of love and healing.

10. Did your lifestyle at any point in your life resemble one or more of these women? Take a moment to revisit these personas and rate them according to their influence. _____

_____

_____

_____

_____

11. What role(s) do you still assume today? How will you begin a vulnerable, more intimate way of relating to your husband? _____

_____

_____

_____

_____

12. *R*ead Romans 8:37-39. How do these verses apply to you or to any woman who feels somehow separated from God? _____

_____

_____

_____

_____

Common Sexual Patterns

$\mathcal{C}$harles and Gayle made love for the most common gender-based reason. He believed sex made him feel emotionally connected to Gayle, while Gayle would rather put off sex *until* she felt emotionally connected to Charles. It's easy to see how, based on that difference alone, the bedroom can be a chaotic mess. We are complicated, both individually and as a couple. To cope with our unique situation, we develop patterns of relating sexually as a couple. Over time, these patterns can become more and more ingrained. Or they change. We're here to look at the patterns from the past and present. We'll evaluate them for their effectiveness at this stage of our marriages.

Throughout this study, we will use the 80/20 Rule, a disclaimer which recognizes that 80% of a particular group will fall into a stereotypical behavior, while 20% won't fit. In other words, though men and women operate biologically and psychologically differently, they cross stereotypical lines of gender because of temperament and numerous mitigating factors.

We also live in a state of struggle against selfishness. The Bible says sin continually "crouches at the door" (Genesis 4:7). Those patterns which arise out of selfishness don't necessarily get better as we age. By recognizing them, we can start to build better ones. This takes effort, communication, intentionality, and purpose. Our goal in this study is to develop fulfilling and energizing patterns in our love lives.

Which of the six patterns below best describes your sexual relationship?

The Caveman Chase

In The Caveman Chase, the husband (i.e. Mr. Caveman) often **sexually pursues** his wife. She doesn't need or want sex as much and possibly doesn't feel turned on by the way he approaches her (*"Really? I just walked in the door!" "You're kidding. I just started dinner."*). Whatever her reasons for lack of interest, reasonable or not, both spouses often live with some level of tension – his sexual frustration and her ambivalence toward his demands. Historically, 80% of American homes have fallen into this pattern.

1. *While* the husband's sex drive has long been the subject of women's complaints, how do you see it in today's culture? Has the media reinforced the Caveman stereotype or debunked it? Explain. _____

_____

_____

_____

2. *If* you lived in this pattern in the past, for how long? Is it still going on today?

_____

_____

_____

The 20% (er, 30%) Club

Some wives desire sex more often than the husband. A woman in this dilemma may unknowingly make her man feel "less than" by her frustration and apparent disappointment if he doesn't meet her needs. She may not know how to express her feelings, partly because of the surprise at finding herself in this situation. *This isn't how it started out! It's not supposed to be this way!* Her disillusionment and sense of rejection may cause a negative cycle of tears, pleading, and eventual withdrawal on both sides.

Sadly, because of the confusion and sensitivity of the husband, her panic and tears only make matters worse. We will discuss the 30% Club further later on, but for now, both partners must recognize that a woman's sex drive springs from her need for deep emotional connection. Sex is never about the sex. It has profound meaning in the female soul, and a husband may not get it – though he can learn. This couple may need help with communication.

3. Are you now or have you ever been the higher drive wife? Use this space to share your journey. _____

_____

_____

_____

_____

_____

Note: The 20-30% Club is growing in our culture partly due to the preponderance of pornography among women. As a wife assumes more leadership roles in the workplace, she may feel social pressure to compete with men. As a result, she may come to view sex as a physical activity rather than a relational one. This may leave both spouses emotionally disconnected in shifting sexual expectations and roles.

4. For which partner do you feel the most compassion – Caveman or 30% Woman? Why? _____

_____

_____

_____

The Distracted Knight

If either of the above patterns continue, the defeated husband may eventually back off sexually. This reaction could lead to porn use, depression, workaholism, obsessiveness in hobbies, or whatever distraction will take his mind off this sense of rejection. At first, the wife may be relieved he's less interested. She doesn't realize, however, he still needs her. She still needs him! Some spouses, tragically, begin an affair under these conditions. Those who remain "faithful" live in a dangerously vulnerable place.

5. *If* this withdrawal happened or is happening in your marriage, or one you know well, tell about it here. _____

_____
_____
_____
_____

"We're Just Fine!"

Sometimes, both spouses not only give up trying to connect, they *settle* into emotional disconnection. With waning hormones, they may stop thinking about sex altogether. The wife busies herself with other projects and leaves her husband to his. She doesn't feel cherished, and he most likely doesn't feel loved or respected. Though they do things together, even have sex occasionally, they don't connect emotionally. This couple may be committed to each other and seem "fine" to the world. They don't fight much. Maybe they've even quit hurting. Maybe…

6. *Is* this you? Give possible reasons many couples live out the last decades of their lives in this pattern_____

_____
_____
_____
_____

The Unhappy Seesaw

In the Unhappy Seesaw, both mates have moments when sex is just the ticket for a fine day or night. They have sexual feelings and find themselves drawn to the other at times. Yet, for some reason, they *can't or won't* happily accommodate each other's needs. When she approaches him, he finds a logical reason to back away. Then later, when he approaches her, she has a ready excuse to decline. They both insist the other just can't pick good times. She firmly declares he only wants her when she *can't* engage. And *vice versa*.

In this pattern, no matter the age, both partners retreat regularly into an emotional stand-off. No fun, no engagement, no resolution. Tension at a deeper level causes a terse calm in the home. Both struggle with fears of intimacy and inability or unwillingness to forgive. Sex, when it happens, isn't fulfilling. The tension lifts for a millisecond, then returns.

This pattern can start when hormones wane and the couple no longer feels a sexual urge. However, the pattern is most prevalent when one or the other doesn't feel worthy of happiness or delightful connection. Shame from abuse or a promiscuous past keeps him or her from accepting God's poured out forgiveness (Bruised Barbara). They can't forgive themselves.

Each of us who believes Christ died to cover the debt of the worst we could ever do, is free. When guilt comes because of what *others* did to us, the battle for Truth is on! We forgive our offender because God forgave us. If we're honest, we're all messes – but the Good News sets us free!

If this is your pattern, run to a trusted friend or counselor for help – and stay with this study. God can meet you in your habit of refusing to forgive yourselves or others, or your habit of thinking joy is for the other gal.

7. *Tell* of a period in your marriage where this Unhappy Seesaw threatened your sexual equilibrium. _____

_____

_____

_____

8. What part does lack of forgiveness play in your willingness to accommodate your mate? Rate on a scale of 1 to 10 the level of unforgiveness in your love life today. _____

_____

_____

_____

The Happy Seesaw

We end with The Happy Seesaw to encourage you with a goal. In this loving, hard-working mindset, each mate freely approaches the other for affection or sex. The dynamic makes sex interesting because there's no pattern of initiation. Both want each other at different times and gladly say yes.

If a couple did little else to keep juices flowing, simply reversing who initiates sex from time makes the seesaw a happy one. Both feel desired. Both feel loved. Both have security and trust in asking for sex. This pattern takes good communication and a sacrificial kind of love. The husband defers to her. She defers to him. They live the mandate of I Corinthians 7:5.

Through the storms of life, this couple blesses the community *and the world* through their unselfish love.

9. List some qualities this wife probably exhibits. _____

_____

_____

_____

4

A Time to Know the Man on the Other Pillow

What Makes Men Tick?

*W*hile Kathy waited for an oil change in a small, semi-crowded waiting area, she decided to pull out her AWE homework and tackle the quiz below. After a few minutes, sensing the man beside her looking over her shoulder, she glanced up at him. He shrugged and mumbled, "I wish *my* wife could take that quiz."

This story made us all laugh as we imagined Kathy's face when she caught the man not just peeking but actually reading the questions! Our discussion then turned to what the man meant by his comment. Do most husbands feel misunderstood by their wives? Do we know what makes our husbands tick? In this chapter we hope to shed light on some generalities as well as your particular man. So this quiz is for both of you.

As you ponder these true-false statements, keep in mind the 80/20 Rule, and that men may change views from season to season. There are no right or wrong answers here. Give it your best shot, then ask Hubby to take the quiz by covering your answers with a strip of paper. He can write his on the strip. Have a great discussion comparing answers.

_____ 1. Sex is all men think about.

_____ 2. Sex is primarily a physical need for men.

_____ 3. To men sex means one thing – going all the way.

_____ 4. Sexual frustration often comes out in floating anger.

_____ 5. Men can throw sex out the window if it's too much bother.

_____ 6. As long as he gets sex, your passive attitude about it doesn't matter to him.

_____ 7. Men don't feel rejection as keenly as women do.

_____ 8. Men respond quicker to visual stimulation than women do.

_____ 9. Lack of testosterone can prevent men from being interested in sex.

_____ 10. Only attractive (or sexually charged) women turn on a man.

_____ 11. Men feel loved when having sex.

_____ 12. Men respond to touch as much as women do.

Based on his answers, how many did you miss? _____ Talk with your small group about how far off you were. Read on for more insights.

Sex From the Male Perspective

After reaching the summit of Mt. Everest, an expert climber was asked about his thoughts on the experience. "Oh, it was exhilarating," he said, "but still not as good as sex." Perplexing? Ridiculous? Understandable? What did you think of his response?

Women want to know why sex is so easy and such a big deal to men. It doesn't make sense apart from a purely practical standpoint – that sex must be somewhat compelling and somewhat biologically uncomplicated in order for our species to continue. We forget how boys' sex organs so conveniently reside outside their bodies. This fact makes them naturally develop a, let's say, close relationship with their body parts even in toddlerhood. Did you observe these behaviors in your little boy and wonder if he might have been different from the rest? Think again.

When puberty arrives between eleven and fourteen, the pituitary gland secretes massive amounts of the hormone testosterone. When this happens, boys may ejaculate in "wet dreams" while asleep. Researchers also find that men of all ages have up to several dozen erections *each night during sleep*. Young men also report random daytime erections which have no explanation – in class, while brushing teeth, or mowing the lawn. Ejaculation (orgasm) is a sensation that's, well… sensational! It's probably a good thing few young girls have any idea all this is going on!

A Time to Know the Man on the Other Pillow

Considering the added design factor which makes men crave emotional connection with a woman, we get to the "big deal" part of the question. The view from the summit of Mt. Everest? The climber seemed to hold a *relational as well as physical* view of sex – which happens to be God's brilliant idea.

1. *A*sk your husband about his early sexual feelings. How did your conversation help him connect emotionally with you? _____

_____

_____

_____

Men need sexual validation at a young age, and the need for it never leaves them. Feminine approval or lack of it drives a constant struggle with fears and doubts about his manhood. Testosterone on the loose in the locker room, on the sports field, and in the corporate conference room, ignites hot competition. As *alpha males* vie for top gun, getting the girl is as much about a man's self-image as the attributes of the girl. All this physical and psychological competition can promote great achievement *as well as* not-so-great insecurity.

Do you see how testosterone fuels both sexual desire and pressure to perform in the great arena of the world? If we women don't embrace the first result of the hormone (a strong sex drive), we are at risk of being left without the benefit of the latter (great achievement); and in that case the world is doubly doomed. For in appreciating *their* strengths we garner an opportunity to partner with our husbands, through *our* strengths, to make the world a better place.

2. *T*hink of a time you saw your man chafe under an offhand comment about his virility? Has he told you a story about this from his past? _____

_____

_____

_____

Most men hide their emotional need for a woman's validation of his manliness. Manhood sees this need as an internal whine or cry. Regarding his fascination of the female form, no such hiding exists. He finds Woman the most fascinating creation on earth and likewise wants her to feel his muscles as he flexes.

3. *H*ow do you affirm your husband's virility on a regular basis? _____

_____

_____

_____

The downside of being the most fascinating beings in the universe? When men fall for the opposite sex, they fall hard. Testosterone, combined with vulnerability to a woman's approval, sometimes makes them react more dramatically to rejection than women do. Depression or misplaced anger often result. A man's masculine identity, so wrapped up in his ability to woo a woman, causes much misunderstanding on our part.

4. *T*ake a guess. What percent of fights/violence in the world might be attributed to sexual or romantic frustration or jealousy? _____

_____

_____

_____

Why Is He This Way?

Marie, a late-forties wife and mother, confessed to the AWE group that her husband's obsession with sex confused and angered her. Why the huge difference between her interest and his?

"He's always in the mood! After coming home from a week-long work trip, he wants to make love — twice a day!" Some heads nodded. She had company.

Barely holding back tears, she continued, "I loved sex the first few years. But when the babies arrived, after each one, my body felt different. Sex hurt at first, but then felt sort of so-so. After a long day of taking care of the kids, I just wanted to sleep! In all this time, I've never gotten back to that happy place..." Marie worried about herself, but even more, she questioned her husband's relentless interest in her body. *Is a man's desire for sex every day or two a good design by a good God?*

As a group, we compared men's sex drive to the rugged mountains of Colorado — a bit daunting, and more appealing from afar. Yet we all admitted to loving *real* men! We don't want milquetoast. We love the thought of being carried up a staircase and lifted onto a tall bed by a super-buff fella who at that moment can't think of anything but us. Why does the *thought* thrill us more than the *reality* of our man panting after us?

Our feminine sex drive is quite different. It resembles a botanical garden or the manicured terraces at a tropical resort hotel. No wonder Solomon compared female bodies to a garden, for we are like a garden in our mind and bodies – and we contain yet another garden in our female parts. Men can't help but be fascinated – especially by the last one. If only he'd be content to just stroll along the rose-bordered lane called Cuddling! And sometimes he is. Yet all the women in Marie's group agreed that a man's anticipated reward *after* the stroll makes him look at it in a different light.

God made men different for important reasons. We see that women's complicated psyches, like gardens, require constant care – to be watered and tended. In other words, talk, non-sexual touch, fun activities, and more talk. This need for maintenance counterbalances his strong desire to sexually connect. As we see how the pleasure of sexual fulfillment motivates men to connect with us mentally and emotionally, we can begin to appreciate the good design of a good God.

Marie's candid frustration opened the door for other women to share a different perspective. Since their husbands had long since given up interest in the bedroom, their homes suffered a sadder kind of stress – depression, business-like conversation, and emotional distance. When she saw the tears in these women's eyes, Marie began to look at her husband through a new lens – God's and his.

Together we reviewed six reasons men are generally more sexually-driven than their wives.

Testosterone Produces Leadership and Protection

Testosterone not only produces the children the world must have to continue, it also ignites a deep care for his greatest treasures – you and your offspring.

Does a man suffer undue pressure in the two roles for which God designed him? Or do you see him fulfill them naturally? The answer has to be yes and no. Testosterone helps him. But sin makes him selfish, his role difficult. That's why we want our daughters to marry a man who loves God and sees his need for help in being the man he should be. That being said, have men quit giving up their seats for women? Do men still put a woman on the inside of a walkway, away from the traffic side? These actions seem to be dying in the present culture of false equality. Yet, when pressed, women want protective, strong men.

1. *T*ell about a time your husband put forth great effort to make you safe or a conversation where he expressed his desire to fulfill these God-given roles.

_____

_____

_____

Testosterone Motivates Understanding of You

We've all heard that old saying, "You can never understand a woman." True, he may not fully understand what you're thinking or going through, but he'll listen to your problems and hurts and hang-ups *if* you appreciate his kind of connecting. A sexual encounter motivates him toward *your* kind of connecting.

2. *R*emember a time when your husband asked you to explain how you felt. Tell about it here. Why do you think he took the leap to understand your heart?

_____

_____

_____

_____

_____

Testosterone Helps Marriage Through the "Glory Years"

Yes, our incredibly adorable children filled our lives with laughter and joy, but we also felt utterly exhausted most of the time. I coined the term Glory Years because everything truly was simpler during that time. We necessarily focused on just a few things, kids and survival. And, we still had estrogen.

So what does this have to do with men's sex drive? Let me explain. When I was a wreck and the house was a wreck, I needed this man's help. I had to realize that his excellent character wasn't the only thing that kept him home when he might have run away to the French Foreign Legion. His need for sexual connection with me often got both of us through the tension of putting the kids to bed. Alone at last, it felt good, peaceful, to fall into loving arms.

Linda Dillow, author of *Intimate Issues and Creative Counterpart*, shares that she marked her calendar twice a week during those "Glory Years": "**TS**" for **Think Sex**. Thinking about sex ahead of time helped her to be ready for hubby when a bunch of toddlers finally fell asleep.

When a woman meets her husband's sexual needs, even while holding sanity by a thread, wonderful things can happen – he may change a diaper or make a sandwich for a small mouth. He may even draw a bubble bath for you! That's a husband's love, my friend. *Your love*, which *he* often spells S-E-X, goes a long way in building a strong partnership in the family.

3. Remember a time you saw this principle at work in your Glory Years.

_____

_____

_____

_____

Testosterone in a Soldier Drives Him During Battle

Besides the powerful draw home to you, this hormone fuels his altruistic desire to make the world a better place by fighting our enemies. Testosterone can make men accomplish almost superhuman tasks under stress. You can probably think of a dozen movies with just this theme. Men – not all men, but the majority – truly are hardwired for war, and this is a wonderful reality.

4. Share a story of this kind of testosterone at work._____

_____

_____

_____

_____

Testosterone in the Later Years
Promotes Emotional Connection

The kids are gone. Life becomes less stressful. Now your relationship needs a boost of male testosterone. For even with nagging health issues and changing hormones, your husband needs your touch every day. He wants you more than he lets on. Your love might even bring him back to the table to solve the many problems which come at this stage of life.

"Let's talk, Honey…" are words some wives never hear. Most men aren't wired that way. But sex may open up his heart to you. On that point, I cornered my OB-GYN doctor while undergoing a pap smear. It's true. I told him about my class during our conference time and said, "I sure would love your advice. What's the most important lesson to teach the women about men?" He said he'd think on that for a few minutes.

I went to the exam room to change. A few minutes later, with my feet in the stirrups and a nurse standing behind him, he finally summed up his thoughts. "Men feel most loved when they are making love. Tell your women to connect with him this way because it is HIS way." And there you have it from my fifty-something doctor, speaking wisdom during a pap smear. He will remain anonymous.

5. Try to remember when your man seemed more ready to solve issues because you connected sexually. _____

_____

_____

_____

Testosterone Nourishes Men's Bodies and Minds

Testosterone gives a man more energy to do things he wants to do. It gives him more confidence and helps his brain problem-solve better. Plus, his sex drive makes him like you more! Unless you've seen the decline of your husband's sex drive or if he's received a low Testosterone blood test, you won't appreciate the importance of this hormone.

Remember the *Law of Supply and Demand?* Let's look at it in light of the high-drive husband.

This law says that when demand in an area is high and supply low, panic can hit an economic system. Just as consumer confidence essentially drives a nation's economy, when supply is high, demand drops. This is true in your sex life. Though it may take weeks or months of your consistency *as a ready partner*, one day he will sense a new stability in the relationship. Watch demand drop. When you turn him down and make a date for the near future, he'll be fine with it; he sees supply hasn't changed. You may even find the guy who used to want sex every time you gave him a sweet kiss turn into one who returns the kiss and, well, just goes back to whatever he was doing. And that's a good day, too.

6. *H*ow have you seen the *Law of Supply and Demand* work in your marriage? Don't mistake this principle as a ply for compliance "just because" you want the demand to go away. We want joy and peace, but not at any price. Communication and love make the principle work. Write your thoughts here.

_____

_____

_____

_____

_____

Father, I want to fully appreciate the way you've designed my man. Help me feel the joy of your design and help me let him know. I realize this may not solve all our problems. I realize we still have issues we need to work through. But for now, help me show him I like the way he is drawn to my body.

In Jesus' Name, Amen

What "Being Relational" Means to Most Men

*W*e know what *relating* means to us. We want our husbands to turn off the TV and talk. We want a regular date night each week. Absolutely. Since guys look at relating differently, we must choose to appropriately adapt – or be miserable. Period. Being relational isn't the same thing to both of us.

1. *L*et's find out what "being relational" means to our husbands. For starters, ask him. Record his response here. _____

_____

_____

_____

We already know sex is relational to men, and we know they appreciate many of the "little relational things" from our survey in Chapter 2. Men might also enjoy our company on a Home Depot run, a weekend fishing trip, or cleaning out the garage. While men have reported all these activities as relational, if we look a bit deeper we'll find two ways which men agree make the marriage a truly "relational" one. After reading this section, share the main points with your hubby over a cool iced tea some evening. Call it research.

We'll begin with *his* kind of touching.

When He Touches You, He Is Being Relational

How do you react when Hubs walks up behind you at the stove and nuzzles your neck or otherwise touches you? Do you flinch or act as though he's objectifying your body? Annoying you for fun? Wanting sex right now? What if he simply wants you to know he finds you attractive and loves you? What if he's just being relational?

Warm touch is relational to men, and affection at any point during the day can be foreplay in his mind. Do you see foreplay as the five or ten minutes preceding lovemaking? He doesn't. He's looking for a warm response when he moves toward you, even if it's not the most convenient time for *a moment.*

Remind yourself that your idea of relational doesn't mean his idea is wrong. It's just different. Jill worked hard at moving closer to her husband and found that her kisses made him want sex right now. This is a common problem, by the way. So what do we think in that moment of confused purposes? Some women think, *well, if just a kiss does that, I won't try that again any time soon.*

Not Jill. What did she do? She found a tricky way around the issue. She chooses a time to kiss her husband warmly when lovemaking is *necessarily* off the table – like as he heads out the door to work or when he opens her car door in a parking lot. Her wise actions relate love to him and serve as foreplay for later.

Will you determine to be more fun? Go with a suggestive remark or tug of a shirt. Enjoy a lingering kiss on the neck even if you'd prefer a quick hug. Accept the former in lieu of the latter and you may find him more willing to meet your emotional needs.

2. Compare his comments and touches of the the first years of marriage to those of today. Is your husband less likely to make these overtures or just as likely? Why or why not? _____

_____

_____

_____

You're not alone if you are amazed at how quickly your husband can become aroused – how he can be reading his Bible and wham! suddenly he notices something under your shirt and makes a salty comment. When you react in that moment with a brush-off or roll of the eyes, he stores those gestures in a mental box.

As your husband ages, your rebuffs make being relational more difficult. The rebuffs pile up over the years, and one day he quits noticing "that something" under your shirt. You don't even notice he doesn't notice. In reality, he's not sure you really like him. I know what you're thinking: How can that be?

3. Counselors have suggested that people need up to twenty positive comments to counteract one negative. If you live in "rebuff mode," what will you do to reverse the situation? _____

_____

_____

_____

In a sense we are our husband's emotional water. Instead of feeling pressured, think of this role as a privilege. Like a plant responds to water, he emotionally thrives with our warm response to his touch. This may seem strange, because if our husband rebuffs **our** hug or touch, we process it differently, more questioning, more communicative. *What's wrong, honey? Are you okay?* But when rebuffed, most men will simply move on. Their egos seem as tender as their sex drive is big.

4. Though our relational tank might be filled through our kids, friends, activities, projects, or extended family, how do you think your husband's relational fulfillment is met? _____

_____

_____

_____

Your positive response to his touch also encourages him toward his best self. When he touches you and looks into your eyes, what if he could see himself as God sees him? While his relationship to God is his business, not ours, I Peter 3:1-4 sheds a new light on the nonverbal influence we have on him.

5. *W*rite the key verse from this passage here and what it means to your relationship today._____

_____

_____

_____

Your attitude toward your husband's male way of relating affects him more than you think. If your husband has become distant or irritable, think about how you respond to his tiniest of overtures. He may have given up. Move toward him again. You may be able to build up his confidence by flirting a little – and meaning it. God has made man to be fulfilled in relationship with his wife.

6. *R*eview the ways your response to his touch is so important. Write four different aspects here. _____

_____

_____

_____

The second relational need of men may surprise you, but whether or not you already know it, now's the time to come to terms with:

The Sight of Your Body (with very few clothes) Is Relational to Him

How do you feel about undressing for your man? Well-known author Gary Smalley voiced for all men everywhere the best way a woman can prepare for lovemaking: show up naked. We laugh an uncomfortable laugh because we think, *Okay, sex is one thing. Putting my body on display, on purpose, like out in the open? Well, that's another.*

In case you didn't know, men have a mental file besides the (collected rebuffs) one we referred to above. In this rolodex-like file, they collect and store images like the photo gallery on our phones. They mentally flip through these photos as they go about their day. The images come from billboards, women they see in public, magazine covers, or the internet. Think about this: If your man is blessed to garner pics from daily life with the woman he loves, his mental gallery might not be stocked with photos from other places. (We will discuss the terrible effects of pornography later.)

Your husband enjoys glimpses of your body even without the prospect of sex. The millisecond view of your semi-naked body as you fumble through your underwear drawer leaves an imprint in his mind all day – one that makes him want to come home. This is how men are built. In Proverbs 5:19, God clearly told husbands to be satisfied by their wives' breasts all their lives. But how can a man be satisfied by something he never gets to see?

7. *When* did you last undress in view of your husband? On that occasion, what did he notice or say? _____

_____

_____

_____

Most women enjoy *dressing up* for special occasions such as a wedding or theatre date. We value his opinion of our outfit. We want him to notice. Why, though, do we *dress up* for the sometimes *elusive* compliment, yet find it distasteful to *undress* for the *sure* compliment? What about you? Do you think: *Isn't my nightgown attractive enough? Just the thought of putting on some sort of show for him seems perverted.* Women report three possible reasons for harboring such thoughts:

a. You feel unlovely even fully dressed – but especially being undressed.

b. You struggle with shame from a past use of your body.

c. You fear he will consider your nakedness a small thing.

The first reason for withholding our nakedness makes sense among women who have passed what they consider their prime – forties, fifties, and beyond. Whether in broad daylight or candlelight, so many of us feel too fat, too saggy, too wrinkled, dimpled, and scarred. Yet, to a man, his wife's body remains beautiful! I must repeat this. Husbands find their wives' bodies sensuous – even with extra pounds. If you feel competition with the standard of perfection promoted by steamy movies and grocery store magazines, of course you feel *less than.* That sense of competing standards has to stop! Let's confront our cultural obsession with the perfect body by seeing our imperfect body through his eyes.

Second, do you feel a sense of shame in showing your husband your body? Nakedness and shame come as a set after the first sin of Adam and Eve. In Genesis 2:25, we read that in the Garden of Eden they were naked and unashamed. It was disobedience which made them suddenly aware of their nakedness and they *became* ashamed. What a strange twist of the open eyes the serpent promised (Genesis 3:5). But because of his grief and great love, God clothed them and instituted a plan of restoration. Know that no matter how you used your body in the past, God has forgiven you through Jesus Christ!

8. *If* you associate nakedness with impurity and ungodliness, tell how it happened. _____

_____

_____

_____

9. *Read* Psalm 34:4-5. Write it in your own words here. _____

_____

_____

_____

_____

Third, most of us have heard the term "emotional nakedness." In traditional literature as well as in the Bible, willful, open physical nakedness symbolizes vulnerability and trust. Understanding the connection between emotional nakedness and the physical kind helps explain a woman's natural hesitancy to undress for anyone, including her husband.

God refers to our body as a temple of His Spirit. Though only a breath away from reverting back to dust, he greatly values our body. He places that sense of value into our very being so we will care for it and radiate his love through it.

Therefore, to force any person to remove clothing violates them at a deeper level – it is an intrinsic, egregious offense. A good man sees not only the value of his wife's beauty open to him, but the sacrifice of her natural modesty in presenting it – a "living sacrifice" as we read in Romans 12:1. Though the verse refers to our body as a living sacrifice presented to God, marriage, by design, reflects and illuminates that relationship. A good man's heart overflows with gratefulness when he realizes the significance of what she offers – and that gratefulness can create a new level of intimacy.

10. *C*opy Romans 12:1 (add verse 2 for extra credit!) as a reminder of our reasonable worship of God. _____

_____

_____

_____

11. *D*o you relate to the fear of being *taken for granted* in your attempts to be vulnerable in this way? How might you address this fear with your guy? ____

_____

_____

_____

Before we mislead you into thinking all nakedness in the home is alike, we must discuss the difference between **relational** **nakedness and the** *familiar* **kind**. Some of the ladies in class said they always sleep nude. Many said they often shower with Hubby – but only to get clean. After one group shared this, I asked my husband, "What do you think? The ladies undress with no problem, but don't see the relational significance in it – to either them or their husbands." His unequivocal answer: there is nakedness, and there is *Nakedness*. In the capital letter word, a wife isn't necessarily fully undressed – possibly just partially – but she wants him to notice. And he sure will.

In the lower case use of the word, however, a husband may not notice her *familiar completely* nude body at all. It depends on how he or she (especially she) spins the moment.

What about you? Do you shower together sometimes just because of a traffic jam in the bathroom? Has his unclothed body become familiar to you in that setting? His body means nothing to you unless you make it mean something. Same with him seeing your body as the years go by. In earlier years, tiny glimpses of you without clothes would turn him on, but not so any more. He wants you to be intentional about showing him your body. In the same vein, you must actually "notice" him without his clothes.

12. $\mathcal{H}$ow will you spin the moment the next time you find yourselves in a naked situation? _____

_____

_____

_____

So... if undressing is particularly difficult for you, don't fully undress in front of Hubby. As you work through the issues in your case of The Cover-Up Blues, be creative. **Follow the progression below.** You'll be undressing, delightfully maybe, before you know it. Some of you need to add these ideas to your playlist, anyway, shy or not!

a. After a shopping trip, tell him you'd like to show him what you bought. Give him a fashion show by removing everything down to your beautiful undies. Now put on the new item or items one by one. When I go thrifting, I usually come home with several things. He'll always stop **whatever** he's doing for my fashion show.

b. Don't struggle with dressing right after a manicure. Ask him to zip up your zippers and button your buttons. Be a little dependent.

c. Come out of the shower or tub in a towel only. Find him, give him a hug, but accidentally drop the towel. You get the idea. Of course pick it up, but put it back on in front of him so he can see the process.

d. Find a corset with a push-up bra attached. Yowzer.

e. Dress normally for bed but draw a little body art on your shoulder or chest for him to discover. (Each husband has his favorite letter in this list. Try them all.)

f. Put together a drawer in your bureau just for sexy clothes you might wear while watching TV or sitting around the house at night. Keep it stocked with things you'd never wear out of the house.

g. Wear a nice conservative apron while cooking, assuming you are alone for this meal. But wear only the apron.

i. Invite him into a tub of bubbles with you. Bubbles make excellent clothes, while they last.

j. Show up to the dinner table or bed wearing only a necklace. Or scarf. Or hat. Or high heels. Or just cowboy boots.

13. Which of the above suggestions will you try first? _____

_____

You have a burning question… have all these ideas been field-tested? Yes, women in our groups do field-test these suggestions. To be completely honest, though, I just thought of the cowboy boots. My husband has a few images in his mental rolodex and I reap the benefit: he fixes breakfast at least three mornings a week!

5

A Time to Talk About Change

Menopause and Its Pesky Leftovers

*T*hink about a lovely afternoon sailing on a smooth lake, warm sunlight breaking the breeze, when suddenly, dark, foreboding clouds roll overhead. *A storm? I didn't see this coming.* Then wham! a blustery squall hits. Winds full of rain and hail rock your boat.

That's my best picture of menopause. The storm began for me at about 45 when my periods changed and became irregular. Anxious feelings came from out of nowhere – and for the first time in my life, sleep evaded me – at night, that is.

A blood test and a talk with my OB-GYN revealed hypothyroidism, a common thyroid deficiency of perimenopausal women. I learned that perimenopause begins when a woman's periods or emotions change in the mid-to-late forties. With synthroid medication, normal periods returned, along with a good night's sleep. But only for awhile. No one prepared me for the 24/7 *Crazy* right around the corner.

At age 47, mental and emotional confusion set in again – only worse this time. The younger kids who still lived at home said, "Mom, you should really get dressed for the *day*, not for the afternoon!" Most days I refused to *groom at all* until the clock told me Hubby could walk in at any moment. Until then, my long, old-fashioned chenille robe clothed me.

The couch whispered a constant invitation. I reasoned, "Hey, if a nap just sits there like a plate of cookies, why not take it?" Then at night, I roamed the house as the world slept. Late afternoons, the kids played happily outside. With no energy to cook dinner, I'd sometimes go to my room, curl into a fetal position and cry. *Am I losing my mind?*

Also, in the middle of the night, something other than Desire caused me to peel off my nightgown – droplets of sweat on my neck! A sign on my bathrobe might have read: "Household Beware! Crazy Mom on the Loose!"

Eight years. The rude visitor from the netherworld rocked my boat for eight long years.

Be assured, though, many women sail smoothly through the passage on calm seas. After a full year with no periods, menopause is over.

Whether you're already through, or hear distant rumblings, use the chart provided on page 82 to record early or late symptoms. The list can also be used to record what other group members found helpful.

Thankfully, many of these symptoms eventually fade. Just as childbirth experiences run the gamut from short and easy to long and horrific, menopause memories do, too – and it's not hard to get women talking about both. Have you ever noticed how quickly women bond through stories such as these? One shares a hot flash moment, another will jump in, and they're off. All meld into one grand commonality: womanhood.

Many years past my own storm now, I can confidently say that menopause isn't the end of vibrant color and vitality. It begins a great new chapter with a different kind of radiance – in many ways better!

In the meantime, let's listen to two women who highlight some of the most troubling issues *related to sexual intimacy during menopause.*

Allie – "I've experienced varying libido cycles in my twenty-five-year marriage – sometimes high and sometimes low – but generally I've been the higher-drive partner. **Sex was always my way of emotionally connecting to my husband.** I knew

Joe cared deeply for me, but his business worries and lots of health issues wiped out his libido while in his early fifties. He just never needed sex as much as I did. He stayed fairly well engaged until menopause symptoms began. During that year my libido *increased!* I wanted sex to fall asleep, but Joe conked out the minute his head hit the pillow. He slept soundly. I fumed.

Soon migraines, insomnia, and mood swings came into the picture. I was miserable in social situations. Before, I liked going out and doing things. Not during that time. I wanted to stay home. Sometimes my headaches lasted three days. The best cure, sex, somehow didn't work out. Of all my struggles, headaches and insomnia attacked my sanity the most. Through it all, even when I tried to explain, Joe seemed disconnected and annoyed at my struggle."

Marge – "I've been married to Boyd for thirty-two years and have always been passive about sex. But he seemed okay with it. He assumed my availability; I pretty much *checked out* during sex and just didn't think about it.

Until menopause hit. Vaginal dryness and way too little foreplay changed the game. **Sex became painful.** One day, even after using lubrication, I hit a wall. I refused to engage saying, 'I just can't. It hurts.' For the first time in more than ten years, Boyd and I fought about sex. He said something had to be done to help with my pain. I would have been happy to quit sex altogether."

These two women exhibited **completely different sexual responses during menopause**. Allie felt weighed down with many common symptoms but needed/wanted sex in order to cope. Marge, however, suffered few symptoms other than vaginal dryness and a worsening libido. If we step back and look at these women, we see a principle at work: **menopause tends to increase issues which already existed**. I call menopause a spotlight.

1. *Has* God shone a spotlight on areas of conflict with your husband? If so, what recurring theme or issue from the past showed up during menopause?

_____

_____

_____

78

Pain, either mild or severe, is a natural reason to avoid intercourse, yet if the discomfort isn't severe, many women continue to have (give) sex. They think it's the right thing to do. Many formerly responsive wives think that because of painful sex they are now somehow failing their husbands. Nothing could be farther from the truth.

2. *W*hat about you? Have you quit sexually engaging as often or stopped completely because of pain? Or do you keep going on as normal, in spite of it? When did changes begin? Share your thoughts about the changes. _____

_____

_____

_____

When our brain associates sex with pain, our libido takes a tumble. Sometimes we don't know which came first – the pain or the libido problem. If sex is painful, you are at the right place. Together we'll discover how women have grown past the problem.

Lubrication is your friend! Just because you never needed additional lubrication in the past doesn't mean you are less sexy now. Buy several brands or types and compare. Try silicone-based (longer lasting and warm), oil-based (eventually absorbs into the skin but also warm), or water-based (colder and long-lasting). Use liberally! Experiment until you find one that works best for you.

3. *W*hat lubrication have you tried? If you haven't tried any yet, do so and report back here. _____

_____

_____

The Pelvic Floor – an important component of our sex lives – is comprised of bladder, sphincter muscle, vagina, and labia – the whole area upon which we sit. Kegel exercises (pelvic squeezes) help build strength in the pelvic floor, thus keeping the uterus and bladder in place as we age. These squeezing exercises also help with painful intercourse by forcing more blood to the area, causing vaginal tissues to plump up and promote lubrication. With pelvic strength aiding the arousal process, pain is less likely.

These exercises can be done while watching TV, doing dishes, or driving. I find that sitting helps engage the right muscles. Are you doing it right? Try stopping the flow of urine when using the bathroom; that tells you if you're engaging the right muscles. When you squeeze, count to ten or twenty, then relax and repeat. Five to ten reps a day will build strength over time; fifty reps a day is a good goal. Not surprisingly, pelvic floor strength feels great to husbands during intercourse. This alone should be enough to motivate you, my friend!

4. *H*ave you tried pelvic floor squeezes, and how have the exercises helped you?_____

_____

_____

As many as one out of four women suffers from **PFD, Pelvic Floor Dysfunction**. In one of the various types of PFD, the muscles around the urinary tract contract and can sometimes constrict urine flow. This causes pain during a flare-up and also interferes with intercourse.

Even without the painful versions of the problem, the pelvic floor naturally becomes weak through childbirth and age. If left unchecked, the uterus and vagina may begin to succumb to gravity, requiring surgery to elevate and reattach affected organs.

Vaginismus, another pelvic floor issue, causes the vagina to automatically close tight when anything tries to enter, preventing intercourse. No one knows what causes these conditions, but in some cases trauma or emotional stresses have been identified. Psychological counseling, exercises, and doctor-prescribed dilators which expand the vagina can help.

During a period of vaginismus earlier in my marriage, I sought help at the library (pre-internet days). I found the following simple technique. With her pelvic floor muscles, the wife tries to push her husband out while he tries to push in. The act of pushing out counteracts the contracting vagina. Since this technique falls under the category of therapy, a husband might have to forgo regular intercourse until the pain subsides. The exercise did help us and permanently cured my short bout with vaginismus.

5. *D*o you have any of the issues mentioned above? How have you dealt with them?_____

_____

_____

Thankfully, a new breed of physical therapists have now come to the rescue! Pelvic floor therapists work with urologists and use highly-specialized techniques, along with exercise, to bring relief for both men and women who suffer in this area.

Finally, in our discussion about pain in sex, we bring up something you hear about all the time: **bone-building and aerobic exercise**. Now is the time to begin an exercise program if you aren't already on one. How will an exercise program help you? The increased blood flow in your core strengthens your heart, keeping a heart attack at bay. Blood pumping in your core builds libido as well as boosts your energy. Your bones need weight-bearing (yes, weights!) workouts to build strength and stave off osteoporosis.

You'll notice how much more you appreciate your body when you vigorously move it. Here are some ideas to get you *off your duff*.

1. Walk a mile or two several times a week.
2. Begin weight-bearing work several times a week. A great international program for building bone strength is "Bone Builders, International." Find a group near you and work out together.
3. Stretch at least twice every day. A fun way to stretch is to have your husband help you. Lying on your back, have him bring your straight leg across your body, keeping your shoulder blades on the floor. Work both sides a few times a week.

As you stumble, walk, or jog through menopause, stay in touch with your OB-GYN, talk about each symptom you add to your repertoire, and explore options. Testosterone sometimes helps libido issues. While Hormone Replacement Therapy (HRT) usually stops hot flashes and night sweats, each woman is unique in her trial-and-error experience with menopause. The discomfort will eventually end. Believe me, better days are ahead!

A Time to Talk About Change

Symptom	How Often or Severe?	Remedy Tried/Date
___1. Decrease in sex drive/libido		
___2. Weight gain/ food cravings		
___3. Painful intercourse		
___4. Loss of skin tone/wrinkles		
___5. Insomnia		
___6. Hot flashes/ night sweats		
___7. Incontinence		
___8. Mood swings		
___9. Depression/ Anxiety/Fear		
___10. Migraines		
___11. Neck/jaw/ inner ear pain		
___12. Fatigue/ loss of energy		
___13. Muscle/joint pain		
___14. Loss of balance		
___15. Memory/ concentration loss		
___16. Increase in sex drive		

Your Thoughts About Your Body Matter

I Peter 3:3-4

"Your beauty should not (only) come from outward adornment
such as hairstyles and the wearing of gold jewelry or fine clothes.
Rather, it should be that of your inner self, the unfading beauty of
a gentle and quiet spirit, which is of great worth in God's sight."

My friend Callie met me for lunch recently. In her fifties, a decade after losing her husband to a heart attack, she reluctantly joined the middle-aged dating scene. Talk about body issues! The photos, the social events, the constant comparisons… she hated it all, and I felt for her. Sure, life in the dating arena can bludgeon self-confidence, but we all hear the same megaphone in our head. It shouts, "Are you pretty enough? Are you pretty at all?!"

In Callie's job as an OB nurse and lactation specialist, she hears women who have just given birth complain, "What in the world has happened to my body?!"

But at her age, she sees things differently. Looking at the crepey skin on her arm next to a patient's young skin, she thinks, *No way around it. I'm getting old!* The mere thought of a potential second husband seeing her fifty-seven-year-old body almost terrifies her. Like me, she's a member of the Post-Menopausal Anti-Gravity Club. Too bad gravity doesn't cooperate!

These thoughts and fears dig a deep mental rut. Like a merry-go-round in the park, recurring thoughts become feelings, and feelings reinforce the thoughts. Around and around... *I'm just not attractive anymore! I'm just not attractive anymore!* Like a centrifuge, the merry-go-round goes faster and faster. Before long, the rider feels sick, but she can't jump off – the merry-go-round must slow down first.

We're here to slow down that merry-go-round of lies and bring it to a complete stop so you can get off. If you can stop the nagging thoughts and see yourself differently, you can enjoy your marriage much more.

1. *W*rite your recurring thoughts (and feelings) about your body here. Start at the top of your head and move down your body._____

_____

_____

_____

_____

_____

2. *W*here did your feelings come from – media, childhood family messages, social situations? _____

_____

_____

_____

3. *D*id you know that 91% of American women are unhappy with their bodies? Only 5% naturally possess the body type often portrayed in the media (source: dosomething.org). Sadly, many of those in the 5% are still not happy with their body. Are you jealous of the 5%? Explain here. _____

_____

_____

_____

4. *How* does the media affect what you think about your body? _____

_____

_____

_____

The media depends on your dissatisfaction with yourself, even demands it. Companies sell billions of dollars worth of products based on our struggle in this area of self-acceptance. If we could see our body as God sees it, much of the "Industry of Discontent" would die. It's time to stop listening to the underlying message: *You can't be truly lovely without buying this.*

5. *What* kind of ads get to you the most?_____

_____

_____

_____

In our youth, our activity levels allowed sugars and high carbohydrates to be processed better – metabolized more quickly for energy. Later in life, we slow down, though not drastically yet. Approaching menopause, we may eat less but choose the comfort foods we crave. Our brain thinks we're starving and tells our body to turn everything we eat into fat. Metabolism changes.

Extra weight is only one of the body image issues with which we struggle now. Our skin sags during menopause, loses its elasticity and plumpness. Both gravity and a lifetime of exposure to the sun take a toll. Oh, the products we buy to reverse this curse! Without vigorous exercise, our muscles atrophy. Pigment-run-amuck deposits dark spots on our arms and back. Our legs develop bulging veins. Our hair thins. Our feet get bunions. Our posture begins to droop. Read Ecclesiastes 8 for Solomon's version of the process.

6. *Where* are you in this process now? _____

_____

_____

_____

God Cares What You Think About Your Body

Under each statement and verse below, write your response to God in a prayer. Ask the Lord to remind you of these truths and to be delivered from the merry-go-round of conformity to this world.

a. I Peter 3:3-4 says "Your beauty should not come from outward adornment such as hairstyles and the wearing of gold jewelry or fine clothes. Rather, it should be that of your inner self, the unfading beauty of a gentle and quiet spirit, which is of great worth in God's sight."

_____

_____

_____

b. Psalm 34:4-5 "I sought the Lord, and he answered me; he delivered me from all my fears. Those who look to him are radiant; their faces are never covered with shame."

_____

_____

_____

c. Psalm 31:30 "Charm is deceptive and beauty is fleeting; but a woman who fears the Lord is to be praised."

_____

_____

_____

d. I Samuel 16:7 "The Lord does not look at the things people look at. People look at the outward appearance, but the Lord looks at the heart."

_____

_____

_____

e. $atan's fall came because of the pride of his beauty. Ezekiel 28:17 "Your heart became proud on account of your splendor. So I threw you to the earth; made a spectacle of you before kings."

_____

_____

_____

Your Husband Cares What You Think About Your Body

7. As you stand before him in your birthday suit, what would he say to you?

_____

_____

_____

How would he complete these sentences? (Ask him if you don't already know…)

• I see you as _____

_____

• I hate it when you _____

_____

• I want you to _____

_____

The World Around You Cares What You Think About Your Body

8. Fill in the blanks with words your best friend would say to you. (Ask your best friend to fill this out if you can.)

• You would improve your love life if you _____

_____

_____

• You show all of us you belong to God when you _____

_____

_____

• You encourage your grown daughters and granddaughters when you _____

_____

_____

_____

9. *D*o I hear the sound of your inner merry-go-round grinding to a halt? **In Psalm 139**, God speaks more about your body. For extra insight, read those verses and write the phrases and truths which you hear God saying specifically to you._____

_____

_____

_____

_____

_____

_____

In Proverbs 30:31, we are told that *charm is deceitful and beauty is fleeting*. That doesn't mean physical beauty is bad; it just fades. It still holds an important place in being a woman. Read on.

How Beauty As You Age Enriches the World

❦

While tweezing almost invisible eyebrows the other day, I drew blood. It reminded me of standing behind my mother's chair at her dressing table, head leaned back on my ribs, while I plucked. Every once in a while I'd grab a bit of flesh and her little twitch would bring my teenage mind back to concentration. I wondered, *Will my skin ever be this loose? So un-elastic, so wafery thin…?*

It seemed my skin became like hers in mere minutes after that memory began to fade. Thick dark hairs all too quickly paled and turned in helter skelter directions. Formerly glowing cheeks practically demanded color. It all happened long before I was ready. I didn't like any of it – the lines, the loss of muscle tone, the dulling complexion. I feared, deeply feared, aging.

Yet, I find myself flourishing in the middle of arguably the longest, and in many ways, most productive season of life!

Let me try to prove it.

A quick sweep through the human lifespan (after childhood) begins with Spring. Though adulthood once began at eighteen, recent statistics find many twenty to twenty-seven-year-olds still living at home. The Pew Research Center data shows that more young adults live with their parents than at any time since 1940, up to 32% of millennials.

So if we delay Spring to twenty-one, life surely gets going. During this season, most of us choose a mate, buy a car, have our first baby, and rent or buy our first home. We also settle on a career, decide whether or not to attend church, and figure out how to set up housekeeping as a couple. At the longest, Spring lasts until the first baby leaves toddlerhood. Though it wants desperately to linger, we'll give Spring a generous twelve years – up to about age thirty-three.

The small, bright green leaves must mature and bear fruit in Summer.

Summer arrives when the second child comes along. I feel the weight of this all-encompassing season just writing it. In this massive role transformation, Boyfriend/Hubby now becomes Provider/Daddy; Girlfriend/Wife now becomes Career woman/Mommy. Life gets complicated, both materially and relationally. Summer may include nice family vacations, but it also brings intense heat. As children humble us, perplex us, and thrill us, the stress of raising a family can make Summer the hardest season.

We'll give seventeen years to Summer, taking us to about fifty.

Fifty, you say?! Oh, but haven't you heard? Fifty is the new forty. While in ages past, we were thought to be "old" by then, not so today. During the time between forty-five and fifty, families adopt babies, movie stars *have* babies, and some brave souls even raise their grandchildren. Also, the unwelcome guest, perimenopause shows up, shakes equilibrium, and often brings marital strife in its wake. So, because of our lingering youth and involvement in child-raising, we will say Autumn begins *after* those difficult years of perimenopause.

Still, we go through Summer dreading Autumn! The joy of moving on to the next stage evades us until we finally arrive and *voila!* right before our eyes, so many perks! With the oldest kid(s) out of the home, parenting pressures taper off. The family goes out in separate directions. Life shifts into a lower gear, slowing down the pace of the previous season. And Autumn has only begun.

When does Autumn end?

In my humble opinion, Autumn can last well into the seventies. Think of the women you know who play tennis, travel the world (on their own two feet, no cane or walker needed!), take dance and sculpture classes, and even tackle college degrees they missed in their youth. They may continue to climb the corporate ladder (or actual mountains), take leading roles in their communities, and teach skills and life lessons they learned along the way. These are real women. We're talking about you, my friend!

I challenge you to do the math. Twelve years of Spring, seventeen years of Summer, and twenty-five full years of Autumn – all before the seventy-fifth birthday bash. Autumn can last almost double the length of Spring and Summer combined! It's the reward for hanging in through the hard years of raising a family or establishing a career. It means freedom to enjoy more options, develop closer relationships in the family.

It is also a great time for your marriage. Let me say it again. Autumn is a great time for your marriage! The two of you can sleep in, eat out at the drop of a hat, travel to exotic places… indulge in all the luxuries which weren't so accessible ten years ago. With so much time to grow and conquer our fears, Autumn deserves a better rap. A recent study showed the two happiest years of life to be sixteen and seventy. Makes sense to me.

I also strongly believe that lovely aging enriches the world. It carries a dignity and grace that youth doesn't hold. I'm not talking about just physical beauty. If a woman's outward appearance becomes her highest priority, she's not only shallow, she deceives herself, and her beauty truly is fleeting (Proverbs 31:30). But, since you asked, here are my top reasons why a reasonable amount of effort toward feminine beauty makes the world a better place.

Our Husbands Appreciate Our Beauty

Whether we dress up or wear yoga pants and a t-shirt, the amazing fact remains: a loving husband can still see us as the young girl he married… a lovely face, a wonderful body (even with a few extra pounds), a winning smile, charm, and wit. What miracle keeps us looking very much the same to him over the years? No one knows – it remains a mystery. Though our husbands may appreciate us most when we're naked, all the fully-clothed creativity and sparkle thrill him year after year after year. Our efforts affect his own sense of manliness, too. He's happier when we're happier and radiate energy and pluckiness.

The Young Who Fear Aging Need to See Your Beauty

Growing older is a fearful thing to most people, but especially to our youth. While we don't fear going to heaven – that will be glorious – living inside a decrepit, stiff, falling-apart body does make us shudder. But why? To resist the inevitable is to declare God's gracious providence over the aging process a lie. For we *will* be wrinkly and weak if we don't die young.

Do I really want to slink out of finishing the work God has for me? Joy means working for his glory until he instructs me to just be still and let others care for me. I pray to be sweet in that position. I pray God will make me a world-class *prayer* when that time comes. I am close enough to smell the Bengay already.

In the meantime, if you have never worn makeup and aren't about to start, that's fine. But if you decide at fifty or sixty to begin putting on a bit of lipgloss, you will likely take off a few years and look perkier.

During a recent trip, I enjoyed meeting 104-year-old Clara in a nursing home. Still able to walk with a walker, she wore delicate pearls, pink lipstick, and a stylish outfit. We found her in the coffee shop chatting to all who would sit and rest awhile with her. Those who saw her smiling face feared growing old a little bit less.

Aging parents remind grown children of their own mortality; they need a model for growing older. Does that mean we should shield our children from our aches and pains? It probably couldn't be done even if we tried. A smiling, warm, and positive mom or grandmother makes young folk more comfortable with life's realities. If we try to look our best, they may love showing us off in public. They may even want to be first to run up and introduce us to their friends.

Workplaces Are Transformed by Mature Beauty

One of my friends worked as a caregiver in a highly stressful environment. Female employees were required to wear fashionable clothes, makeup, and a stylish haircut. Though these habits didn't make them more productive workers, they did communicate a sense of confidence and professionalism. Thus, they became more effective, commanded more respect from those under their charge.

Beauty helps make the workplace more pleasant. Proverbs 31:30 clearly praises a woman who fears the Lord. Can she be both beautiful and praiseworthy? Of course. The second one simply lasts a lifetime. While she fears the Lord and honors him, her radiant appearance puts the icing on the cake of her service to others. It shows her awareness of her femininity. She reflects his beauty in her beauty. What a way to show the world your faith!

Society Sees God's Design for Sex in Your Wholesome Beauty

Nothing reflects the sexual dynamic of marriage like a couple in love. So what does this have to do with beauty? A few years back, my hubby and I were touring in the Garden of the Gods in Colorado. An older couple, each with white hair, suddenly zoomed by us in a red convertible. Her scarf blowing in the wind and their smiles gave me a picture I treasure. "That's us in ten years, Honey!" I said. They drove past so quickly, their actions had nothing to do with my impression. It was her face smiling beside him.

What does this mean? Whether with her husband or alone, shopping or working, a woman's glowing countenance shows the world the dynamic I admired in that couple. Does feminine beauty flourish apart from marriage or sex? The quick answer is yes. But a woman who cherishes her identity as a woman leaves a whiff of perfumed elegance wherever she goes. We can't separate femininity from sexuality because God created male and female to separately, uniquely, reflect his delight and fulfillment in the Trinity. When a woman radiates a wholesome joy in her loveliness, that's a sermon the world needs. Do you know your beauty, both inner and outer, preaches a sermon about aging?

Father, I want to be a radiant example of fearing you so I can be praiseworthy. I want to pray more than primp, listen more than talk, and give you total credit for any loveliness in my life. Thank you for making me a woman. Help me be joyful in it.

In Jesus' Name, Amen

6

A Time to Choose Your Hormone

Hormones Schmormones!

$\mathcal{W}$ouldn't you think after the menopause storm passed, a girl could catch a break? Yeah, me too. But in 2003, breast cancer made its appearance – a much bigger storm in many ways. Because my breast cancer was the **estrogen-receptive** kind, my doctor explained that estrogen is now bad for me. Even after ovaries stop producing the female hormone, *fat cells may* produce enough to feed microscopic cancer cells. So, when two years of surgeries and cancer treatments ended, I began an **anti-estrogen pill** to prevent production of the cancer's fuel.

One day toward the end of treatments, my husband asked the doctor, "When can we say we are cancer-free?"

"Right now," she responded. "Go ahead. Live life and put all this behind you. We went after the disease with all guns blazing."

Ahhh… finally post-cancer at fifty-six, physically strong, it felt great to enjoy aerobic exercise again. But, at the very time my libido might have made a welcome comeback, it completely flatlined. A diary of my interest in lovemaking would have read the same every day: *no interest, no interest, less interest.* My oncologist and gynocologist offered little help. Exercise, check. Lots of water, check. Able to tolerate my husband, check. No, I liked him – a lot – as much if not more than before. Check, check.

Sad, but mostly befuddled, I began to study libido under the cloud of a hormone-deprived life. I needed answers! Some authors suggested food like oatmeal or chocolate or oysters. But all these aphrodisiacs failed to provide bedroom enthusiasm – only unneeded calories! Most authors, however, did line up on one point: We have to circumvent feelings and choose to operate on thinking. The desire for a zippy marriage spurred me on to be proactive in my thoughts.

A year into the anti-cancer meds, my interest in sex began to grow. I'd learned how the body works with and without hormones. During the second year of the meds, I saw an even greater improvement. And when we began the small groups, I also learned how much company I had out there.

In AWE class, our surveys from Sexually Stuck Women (Chapter 2) confirmed findings from my reading. Women consistently reported pain during sex, feeling unlovely, and low libido. Though libido issues arise from a thousand factors besides lagging hormones, we all agreed that the way we think is a huge factor in libido.

However, before we dive into what we can do to help ourselves in the area of desire, it helps to know basic differences between men and women in general. Most women appreciate learning the following gender characteristics are pretty much universal.

Men	Women
Sex leads to feelings of love	Feelings of love lead to sex
Quickly aroused and satisfied	Slowly aroused and satisfied
Best part is tension release – the Goal	Best part is tension build-up – the Journey
Wants quick direct stimulation in one place	Wants touch all over – delay direct stimulation
Wants sex in order to relax	Must relax in order to have sex
Aroused visually	Aroused by emotions/sensations
Sexual prime is late teens, early twenties	Sexual prime is thirties and forties
Desire dependent on constant hormones	Desire dependent on changing hormones
Capable of single orgasm at a time	Capable of multiple and varied orgasms

Used by permission from *Passion Pursuit* by Linda Dillow and Dr. Juli Slattery[1]

A Time to Choose Your Hormone

Three Separate Brain Functions

Many people think of sex as one big hormone-induced "high" when we make love. If only it were that simple. Actually, three completely separate brain functions operate in sex: **Attraction**, **Arousal**, and **Climax**. Scientists find these to be separate neural pathways influenced by, but operational apart from, a hormonal push. In other words, sex hormones assure the human race will continue, but our brains can carry on the three parts of sex quite adequately without hormones. Doubtful? Read on.

It all begins with **Attraction**. When I taught first grade right out of college, one particular reading group assembled in a hullabaloo of arguing, pushing, and shoving. School had begun without issues like this so far, so I asked the group, "What in the world is going on here?"

The children pointed to one little boy. He held the seat beside him and almost ferociously announced, "No one sits here but her. She's my girlfriend."

Long after the above experience, my own six-year-old *fell in love* with a nineteen-year-old young woman at church. How did the smitten boy get smitten? We have no idea. But on the night we met this young lady, she leaned forward in her pew and whispered to my husband, "Your little boy just turned around and winked at me."

1. *L*ook back at a time when your child had a *crush* at a young age. _____
   _____
   _____
   _____

Thankfully, because these feelings spring from a different part of the brain, they aren't naturally sexual. Whether mild fascination or a strong craving for the person's presence, crushes on teachers or friends lead to healthy attraction and attachment later. Parents' tender listening helps them process the volumes of confusing messages coming from their own minds as well as the culture. With our son, we walked a thin line between making him feel strange or wrong – and condoning his crush.

In my junior high years, I cultivated crushes like a prize-winning garden. Oh, how I dreamed of them! I still remember two teachers – my tall, brown-eyed science teacher and the gravelly-voiced, prematurely-gray history teacher. I can go back there and feel the feelings, how each one held me spellbound – their smiles, their cologne, the way they moved. During a test once, it didn't take much nerve to approach the science teacher's desk with a question – just for a chance to see those eyelashes.

The fundamental components of attraction for me? Cologne and eyelashes.

2. *How* were crushes a part of your young life? What were your particular components? _____

_____

_____

_____

_____

Attraction in adulthood and marriage is a whole different animal.

Romantic feelings which attract you to your mate, those tingles, *twitterpations*, and desires, are fickle little rascals. If only the feelings could stay. When spouses can't seem to resolve a fight or feel bored with each other, the rift can cause a scary sense that attraction isn't just fading but totally disappearing.

Premarital counseling can help prepare young couples for the inevitable: attraction comes and goes. After years of fluctuations, when hormones of desire wane, attraction so often rules whether or not they will make love. Why? It's the way of least resistance. Our sex-saturated society makes attraction king, giving it the highest place of honor in the game of romance. Books and articles often focus on this one aspect of courting as if, without attraction, relationships will starve and die.

Attraction feels so good, granted, but we must address the conflict between commitment and attraction. These two archenemies meet on the battlefield of every grocery store checkout and media outlet. Magazines tout *just-met-sex* – blissful ignorance of the other person's flaws – as the best sex. Their message is clear: attraction makes sex worthy of pursuit.

When we think of attraction as something that *happens to us*, like *falling* in love, we set ourselves up for misery. In order to grow into a sexually mature person, we must see attraction as a garden we plant, water, and nurture in our marriage. Back in the teens, with those early hormones raging, we didn't have to work at it. Now, however, hormones can be trumped by fights, moods, kids, work, disappointments… you get the picture…

Not if, but *when*, hormones let us down, we can call on our imagination, memory, and education about our bodies to nudge us toward sexual engagement. In his book *Undefiled*, Harry Schaumburg[2] introduces the concept of spiritual maturity as a prerequisite to sexual maturity. He goes so far as to say both kinds of maturity depend on the other. In other words, to be spiritually mature, we must see sex as much larger than our passing feelings, more as a sacrificial way to communicate deep commitment and solidarity with our mate.

3. *How* important is feeling emotionally drawn or visually attracted to your husband before you engage sexually?_____

_____

_____

_____

4. *Rate* the spiritual and sexual maturity of your marriage. Of yourself. On a scale of 1-10, tell how close you are to where you want to be. _____

_____

_____

_____

_____

5. *Have* you heard of or known people in their seventies, eighties, or nineties being attracted to someone? It happens every day. Tell of someone you know.

_____

_____

_____

_____

Arousal, the next part of sex, moves the center of interest to the genital area.

Just as with attraction, arousal also has no known age of origin or ending. Arousal happens in the brain with suggestion, either verbally or visually, and/or stimulation of the body through touch. Though progressive in nature, the process of arousal can be stopped at any level of intensity. Arousal appears in physical signs like increased body temperature, quickness of breath, slight swelling of breasts; but most importantly, it shows up as a pleasant sensation in the groin area.

As a side note, we must teach these things to our children, no matter how awkward. Why? Because if children knew how predators work to groom their prey, they might be better equipped to catch any kind of suggestion or progression as it happens. Not that child abuse would, in this way, stop; but kids would know how their bodies work from a cognitive, scientific, as well as a God-designed perspective. This education can't be undersold!

Since the male body produces much more testosterone than the female body does, we see differences in their natural reactions to arousal. Women seem better able to control feelings; men struggle to control them. When a woman marries, she must choose to allow arousal; the husband must fight his while waiting for her to catch up!

Our minds are capable of ruling the arousal process. Isn't that amazing? In the act of lovemaking, every square inch of skin is engaged, but the mind is the most important sex organ. In other words, sensations on the skin may lead to arousal, depending on how the brain interprets a touch. The mind allows the body to fill with all-consuming feelings of desire. Who could have thought of that, other than our God?

6. Understanding arousal as a progressive function of the brain, how does your mind *interrupt* arousal in your response to your husband? Rate your welcome of arousal from 1 to 10. _____

_____

_____

_____

Climax is the natural end of arousal, but did you know it's a separate brain function?

As arousal continues to build an intoxicating kind of tension, blood collects in the genitals, causing a dense congestion. When the congested blood releases out of the area, the incredible experience of orgasm takes place. This euphoric feeling is a kind of "letting go."

Even though the progression of sex naturally brings orgasm, women can short-circuit its progression at the verge of climax and stop it. Men can easily reach a point of "no return" where almost nothing can stop what is about to take place – ejaculation.

For women, we call orgasm a skill, and it passes through ups and downs over the years. Be encouraged. When arousal short-circuits, creating a minefield of emotional issues, remember, *if the brain or some outside detractor doesn't stop arousal, orgasm will take place.* What an amazing design by our Creator! We'll come back to this in more detail later.

7. *How* do you feel about what you've just read? What did you learn? How will this information help you grow in your marriage?_____

_____

_____

_____

_____

_____

_____

_____

Does Sex Change With Age?

God made the "muscle" of sex able to reactivate after a dry spell, yet you might wonder if a long abstinence means more difficulty in bringing it back to life. Possibly not. Why? Because a couple can work through the three parts of sex one at a time. Read on for a short primer about the three parts of sex.

Since our intricate design allows orgasm to continue throughout life, way past menopause, we can truly exclaim, "Hormones, schmormones!" When the possibility of children is past, lovemaking replenishes a bubbling well of emotional intimacy in the safety of commitment.

By *dating* and wooing, activating imagination, **attraction** gets the process going. **Arousal** usually goes into action when kissing and touching ensues. Then, whether or not **climax** has been a part of life before, the brain can learn or relearn it. Sex doesn't have to be tricky after a long pause. Each couple's attitude, motivation, communication, and education will determine how easy the transition.

Physical limitations notwithstanding, sex can get better with age! Author and researcher Tim LaHaye explains in his book, *The Act of Marriage After 40,*[3] in early marriage, sex is 80% hormonally-driven and 20% love-driven, but later in marriage, it is only 20% hormonally-driven and 80% love-driven. Think about it. Doesn't the latter reality have a better ring to it? Interviews with thousands of older couples reveal that sex may not happen as often, but it can be even more satisfying than in earlier years. Love always makes for better sex.

*W*rite a prayer asking God to bring you into his kind of mature thinking about your sexual relationship. Tell him how you feel today and how you need his help in changing your attitudes.

_____

_____

_____

_____

_____

_____

Oxytocin and My Love Life

Psalm 16:11
"You make known to me the path of life;
in your presence there is fullness of joy;
 *at your right hand are pleasures forevermore."*

As we've seen all along, God's design is beyond understanding – his ways, his provision for us. We wonder why God would create hormones for pro-creation and pleasure and decide to use the same ones to build bones, help us think, improve muscle tone, and provide bright skin. Something feels wrong with this picture. Since testosterone, progesterone, and estrogen do so much for us besides create desire for sex, it seems extremely sad that our bodies stop producing them before our journey on earth is anywhere near over. Have you ever thought to question God along these lines?

Yet, we know we won't live forever in these bodies. Perhaps part of the answer lies in the fact that Adam's sin caused death, and ever since then, our bodies begin to die the minute we're born. Certainly, the exit of sex hormones hastens the many and various ways we slow down.

However, God is fully good! In his goodness he provided oxytocin, dopamine, adrenaline, and many other hormones to regulate and aid our bodies through the aging process. In this chapter, we learn how an especially important one, oxytocin, continues to enhance pleasure until we die.

Oxytocin, known as **The Bonding Hormone**, plays a huge role throughout our lives. During pregnancy, large amounts (as well as progesterone) pump into the mother's body to prepare for childbirth. In labor, it causes the uterus to contract and the cervix to open, allowing a human being into the world. Oxytocin also allows the *letdown* of milk during breastfeeding. But you've heard only the beginning of the story. In the mini-version of my own experience with oxytocin, I hope you'll see how we can tap into this hormone.

During the early weeks of my first pregnancy, after a week or so of spotting, my body became racked by painful labor. Fever and chills took over as one contraction rolled into another. I knew I was losing the baby. Besides being on vacation when it started, I was terrified because I had no idea why or how a miscarriage could cause so much pain.

Only a year later, however, I joyously and *calmly* entered labor for my first full-term child. What was the difference? During the miscarriage, without education, I was *frightened*; in my subsequent labor, I had *educated myself*. By reading about how oxytocin worked in my body, I was able to interpret the sensations of labor as pleasant, not painful. I knew oxytocin simultaneously began labor *and* created in me a sense of euphoria. Over the course of our marriage, I suffered three more miscarriages with varying amounts of labor; but God granted us four wonderful full-term births, all *with minimal pain*. Because I put this powerful hormone to work for me, I can tell you about it. And believe me, there's much more!

Oxytocin works not only to promote maternal bonding after the birth of her babies, it promotes all forms of bonding, including sex. Without realizing why, many a wife has actually told her counselor, "I'd rather cuddle my two-year-old than have sex with my husband." She doesn't realize the same oxytocin which floods her brain while hugging her baby also floods her brain during each part of sex. Education and attitude make the difference. Isn't it great to know that long after the sweet season of nurturing children ends, you can enjoy similar sensations in a different form for life?

Let's look at oxytocin in all three parts of sex. In **desire and attraction**, the tingly feeling doesn't fall out of the sky when we need it. Oxytocin works differently. We have to do *something* to get it flowing. Oxytocin is a chemical which *reacts to a stimulus*. As such, we can make it release into our system by hugging, kissing, and otherwise *warmly* relating to our mate. The best way to ensure an oxytocin release is through a full body hug along with a lingering kiss. David Clarke, in his hilarious book *Kiss Me Like You Mean It*, tells us to take a hug and kiss to the next level.[4]

> ...*take your lover in your arms. A full-body, all-the-right-parts-touching, sensual hug is part of a great kiss... So many spouses pull back so fast from a kiss that they run the risk of whiplash.*

Sometimes it takes eight to ten seconds for a hug to start the flow of oxytocin. As neurotransmitters in the brain receive the message, bonding occurs in those moments. Do you ever shrug off a husband's hug? Instead, what if you reciprocated with a hug, a smile, and a sensual eight-second kiss? You just triggered oxytocin, my friend!

1. *W*hen was the last time you experienced a warm, tender feeling through a non-sexual embrace with your husband? Tell about how you responded to those feelings. _____

_____

_____

_____

_____

If you were to explain this concept to your husband, do you think he might be willing to slow down and enjoy a non-sexual oxytocin moment? Before you answer with a definite no, think of a definite maybe. Most guys love a foot rub, so try this exercise as an experiment. Sit beside your husband or at a right angle to him, remove his shoe and sock, and massage his foot. Within about ten seconds, his brain will secrete oxytocin into his body. He might feel it in his chest or core as a pleasant warmth. As his arm and leg muscles begin to relax, he has no idea what happened – it's just good.

Though able to block or override the above reaction due to stress or some annoyance, he may still have a flow of oxytocin for a few minutes. If he wants to move into sex, (yup, a natural response) tell him you'd like him to enjoy this foot rub for five more minutes. Ten bucks says he'll start to relax, maybe even doze, and forgo the sex.

During **Arousal**, don't rush. Try to slow way down. If you do, oxytocin will make foreplay much more thrilling. Engage as many senses as you can – candles (visual), music (hearing), soft sheets (touch), perfume, chocolate – you get the idea. Oxytocin needs either an outside stimulus or memory to activate. Use your imagination to remember wonderful times you've had in the past.

In the awesome experience of **climax**, oxytocin floods the brain. Different from dopamine, which rises during strenuous activities as well as during sex, the brain can be trained to relish the more sedate, yet powerful, oxytocin. Sometimes it will remain in the system for many hours after a satisfying sexual encounter. Isn't God's design amazing? Will you provide your marriage the nourishment of daily oxytocin?

2. *How* will you increase the production of this hormone in your love life?

_____
_____
_____
_____
_____

The "pleasures forevermore" mentioned in our opening verse are, of course, way broader than sexual. Unlike our husband, our Father provides all our needs, including joy, grace, faith, hope, and enduring love. Use the bonding hormone he provides to indulge in the delights of your marriage. Then give praise and glory to God for his provision.

A Tale of Two Saturdays

This isn't really a "tale." It's a true story of two consecutive Saturdays in the lives of an actual couple. Pseudonyms will hopefully protect the innocent. As you compare the two days, remember, nothing significantly changed from one week to the next. After reading this account, answer the questions about the two Saturdays in light of waning hormones.

Saturday A

At 8:10, Martha woke up to a dark room – alone. A cloudy, drizzly fall morning. *Of course, he's been up for awhile now, reading the news probably. What a great day to sleep in, maybe even all morning.*

The delicious thought of her favorite way to bond played in her mind as she drifted off. Just maybe Chad would go for it. Hardly a millisecond passed before he stood over her with a cup of water and her two morning pills. *That was fast.*

"Here, Babe, but you don't have to wake up yet. Relax. I'll fix breakfast in about half an hour." Chad loved to make eggs and grits lately, especially since she'd hurt her wrist.

"Would you bring it to bed, Honey? I'd love that…"

In the past decade of weekends, he hated to either stay in bed past 7:30, or get back in, once out. How she missed their past occasional Saturdays dedicated to *luuuv!* "All couples need a therapy day," she always said. That meant bedroom door locked, breakfast in bed around 10 a.m. Ahhhh…

This morning he saw "the look"– her demur demi-smile – and added bacon to the menu. At the appropriately late hour of 9:00, he brought the tray to their bed, strawberries sliced and lined up, neatly overlapped. She giggled.

"Yeah, I did that so the blueberries would stay on their side of the plate."

"But, it's reeeeally romantic, Honey."

From 9:30 to 11:00 they alternately chatted, cuddled, and dozed before unexpected sunshine prompted a last-minute decision to check out the local resales. The rest of the day looked like this:

12:30   Burger at Mickey D's, head home with a few purchases.

1:30   Sitting on the bed, Chad enjoys Martha's fashion show of her purchases.

2:00   Martha joins Chad in bed for making out with all the benefits…

3:00   Serious Nap.

4:00   Both wake up, shocked at the time, fall back to sleep.

5:30   Chad wakes up, pours wine, slices cheese, thinks about supper.

6:45   Both swipe crumbs out of bed, think about supper in animated conversation.

7:30   Martha scrounges in fridge for leftovers – serves in bed.

8:00   Both watch basketball on tv – laugh – still in bed.

9:30   Cuddle, continue afterglow with more…

Saturday B

The following Saturday, same couple, normal week.

7:30   Martha wakes with slight headache, looks up without a word at Chad with pills and water.

8:00   Martha goes down to Chad's office, mumbles, "I'll make breakfast in a few."

8:30   Eggs, grits, toast in silence. He suggests a nap "like we did last week." Martha says, "Okay, I'll work on this headache, do some writing… say 4:00?"

Chad replies, "4:00 it is."

9:30 to 11:00   Martha writes emails, forgets to get dressed.

11:45   Chad says, "I have to get a ceiling fan for upstairs."

Martha answers without eye contact, "Wait till after lunch."

12:00   They eat grilled cheese in silence.

12:45   Chad, home with fan, begins what he thinks will be an hour-long project.

3.20   Chad yells down the stairs, "I'm going crazy here! This wiring is all messed up and there's no way I can fix it the way it needs to be."

Martha responds, "No problem on my end, Honey, I'll just keep writing."

4:20   Neither one acknowledges the clock. Chad slumps into a chair in Martha's office. "I'm totally frustrated." He goes to the kitchen and pours a couple of cokes and sets some crackers on her desk. "How's your headache, Honey?"

Martha wonders what his question means. *Is he interested? Does pouring a drink mean let's switch gears? Or did his 'I'm frustrated' comment mean he's abandoning 'the plan'?* When she answers she tries to be upbeat. "Oh, much better, Babe. Sorry about the project … you tried… want to go take that nap?" No answer. They launch into oddly disjointed conversation about the house, dinner plans, etc.

5:00 Chad announces, "Okay, let's get out for a quick burger and go to bed early." Martha sits on her side of the booth and muses. *He didn't have 'the look' when he poured her the soda. What happened to our day, to our special time? What's wrong with us? What does he mean by, 'Let's go to bed early'? But I just don't feel like asking him.*

They drive the short trip home.

7:10 Washing up, teeth brushed, once in bed, they hardly look at each other. Neither makes a move. In one minute, twelve seconds, Chad's asleep. Martha gets up. "Where are you going?" Chad mumbles.

"Don't know... certainly not falling asleep before 8:00."

What do you think?

1. On Saturday A, what did each one do to promote the production of oxytocin?

_____
_____
_____
_____

2. From Saturday B, list three ways each one killed oxytocin production?

_____
_____
_____
_____

3. How will you incorporate a Saturday A into your life? _____

_____
_____
_____
_____
_____

Health Benefits of a Good Sex Life – A Challenge

Hebrews 13:4
"Let marriage be held in honor among all,
and let the marriage bed be undefiled."

Why did she ever-so-slightly glow? My good friend Leah and I enjoyed a cup of tea and chatted about our grown kids and the latest projects in our houses. I kept looking at her face. Serenity. No special makeup… no new haircut. What seemed different?

A half smile crossed her face as she headed down the steps in our last tidbit of conversation. She said something about not getting to bed very early last night. And that's the moment I figured it out. What fun to see the countenance of a sixty-something woman who, when pressed, did admit to a rather special evening!

Are you skeptical about the effect of pleasant (not necessarily rocket-launching) sex on your overall well-being? You're not alone. Yet, no one argues with the connection between our health and a thousand other things we do. Most people see a good sex life as nothing more than an emotional bonus.

A popular women's magazine reported several years ago that scientists somehow determined the increase of happiness from upping sexual activity to once a week equaled the overall feelings of a $15,000-a-year salary raise. How they came up with that number, who knows? But they made their point. Survey results were clear. Regular sex makes us happier.

But health benefits? The professionals agree again. Science (God's idea) shows a clear correlation between a good sex life and the overall well-being of our body. Below are nine health benefits of a robust sex life.

1. Sex helps keep your immune system working well. Studies show that frequent sex produces a substance in the body that increases its *ability to fight infection*.

2. The more sex, *the better libido*. It increases elasticity of tissues in the vagina, helps lubrication, and solidifies the structure of the pelvic floor by use of those muscles. It builds pelvic floor strength, *improving bladder control* through the aging process.

3. Studies have shown that frequent sex *lowers systolic blood pressure* – the first number in your count.

4. Sex can *count for exercise*, depending on your exertion level. It uses about five calories per minute – four more than watching TV. Not too bad for exercise if sitting around is the alternative.

5. Sex *lowers the risk of heart attack*. Exercise is good for your heart, and studies have shown that sex gives the heart a great workout.

6. Sex *lessens pain*, not just by distracting you from it, but by releasing pain-relieving substances into the body. Author Tim LaHaye reported in his book, *The Act of Marriage After 40,*[5] that his wife's doctor ordered lots of sex to help improve her crippling rheumatoid arthritis. Apparently, the chemicals secreted in the body during sex could actually lubricate the joints to make her able to move more freely. They obediently did their homework into old age…

7. In some studies, men who engaged in regular sex were shown to have *better prostate health* and possibly reduced risk for prostate cancer.

8. Sex *improves sleep*. After sex, prolactin is released into the body. This produces relaxation and sleep.

9. Sex can *relieve stress* by the same method. Oxytocin both bonds and relaxes. Reach for your hubby when stress takes a toll. Bonding returns your energy and joy.

The Challenge

Are you ready to meet a real challenge with some possibly observable results? On a designated calendar (or your phone), put a star next to the days you enjoyed sexual activity. Now fill in the following survey and read The Challenge. After finishing the challenge, revisit the survey questions. You may see improvement in your health!

Your baseline question: How often do you presently engage in any sexual activity with Hubby?_____ (Not necessarily intercourse)

Now rate each health question 1-10 (10 being best):

_____ 1.   How am I sleeping lately?

_____ 2.   How is my digestion? Normal BMs?

_____ 3.   What is my energy level?

_____ 4.   How well do I respond to stress around me?

_____ 5.   How is my confidence in problem-solving?

_____ 6.   How is my short/long term memory?

A score of 50-60 is excellent. 35-50 needs some improvement. Below 35 – read on.

If you answered "less than once a week" to the first question, take steps to increase your sexual activity over the next month. **That's the Challenge.** For example, if you've been engaging only once every two weeks or just "taking care of hubby" each week, start mentally and purposefully engaging **for your own pleasure** at least once a week, or more.

After a month of sexually engaging more often, take the survey again. See if your numbers improved. Aren't you curious to see if they do? Don't you want to know if God's design for sex means a better life for you? Those of you over fifty-five may see more obvious results. Why? Because our bodies need care now more than ever. Oxytocin makes a bigger difference in our health! God shows us how the oxytocin provided by sexual activity in later years of marriage mysteriously holds greater significance.

Pray this prayer as you consider taking the challenge starting today.

Dear Father,

I'm skeptical of this challenge, and I wonder if it actually comes from you. But I do see you have made sex good for us. Help me focus on the pleasant results of enjoying your design. Thank you for giving me my husband. Thank you for allowing us to enjoy the delights you have provided for us. Help me follow through with this challenge.

In Jesus' Name, Amen

7

A Time to Help Your Man

In Sickness and in Ever-Changing Health

Colossians 3:12
"Put on then, as God's chosen ones, holy and beloved, compassion, kindness, humility, meekness, and patience, bearing with one another..."

In the opaque light of dawn, before any normal person should be awake, I smelled coffee and stumbled to the kitchen. Mug in hand, I spotted my husband sitting on the patio. His mother's love of birds, alive in him now, often drew him out to hear their early morning songs. As the sun crept over the horizon, I stood in the doorway for a moment. His cargo shorts and yellow T-shirt looked good to me – like in candlelight. When I approached him and laid my hand on his shoulder, he barely moved.

"I'm not the man I used to be, Hon..."

Though my first impulse was to pull a chair close to him and say, "No, Honey, you're a *better* man than you used to be," I held my tongue. I knew *he knew* what he could still do at seventy – climb ladders (though he shouldn't), fix the lawn mower and all manner of other things, run our small business, manage our financial affairs. *But should I remind him?*

No, I needed to listen. Just listen.

Here sat a man who openly struggled with his real and perceived limitations. Less energy. Less accomplished in a day. Less strength. Though he never *did* leap tall buildings in a single bound, he wasn't that former he-man. I don't even remember if that morning fell before his prostate cancer diagnosis or after. Doesn't matter. On this day, his willingness to be vulnerable left an ache in my chest. I realized he needed my confidence and encouragement more than ever.

At the same time, the depth and breadth of his war against aging took me by surprise. It ran deeper than my own struggle. While I dealt with floppy skin under my arms, wrinkles, and disappearing lips, his core identity seemed to hang in the balance.

I remembered our vows… the now obsolete ones once used in wedding ceremonies. "…for better or for worse, for richer or for poorer, in sickness and in health…" Were those words dropped from use because they're too hard? I'll admit, I have sometimes hated those vows. I didn't like the "poorer" part, and I didn't enjoy the "sickness" part – being his care-giver when he was sick.

The worst part for men is when sexual function changes too.

I remembered how AWE classes began with a passion to help women like me see, really see, that we can be our husband's lover despite health issues which threaten our love lives. To see that our husband's needs aren't carnal or petulant, but provide us an opportunity to be more like Christ, to move emotionally closer when life gets tough. For all men hate the reality of aging. The mental part of it colors the physical part, casting a gray shadow on things which might otherwise be taken in stride.

Three of our class members illustrate how a husband's health problems can affect the marriage. In this chapter we will find many ways to lighten the burden of his aging. As you read the true stories below, one of them may have a familiar ring to it. Be prepared to discuss and answer questions about each one.

Katie

Night after night, Katie sat in class without comment. Though I wanted to approach her during a break, I decided to wait. From her brief bio on the first night we learned that Katie and her military husband had lived in various countries. His job as a munitions expert fulfilled him.

Halfway through the class, Katie finally opened up a bit about her worries. In the past, she came home from her hospital job to a normal guy excited to see her. But when he retired from the military, his civilian job fell far short. Strenuous gym workouts helped him cope, but when shoulder and knee pain halted his routine, he began to pull away from Katie. He stopped kissing and rarely initiated sex. "I don't think he's depressed," she tearfully told us, "but whatever is going on with him, I have no libido of my own left. I need *him* to make moves, or at least seem interested."

1. A husband's health problems, combined with other issues, can result in diminished sex drive. How can you relate to Katie's situation? What might you say to encourage her? _____

_____

_____

_____

Julie

Ten years younger than Katie, Julie came to class concerned about her response to her husband's health problems. Following his recovery from knee surgery, still in his late forties, he developed complications. Julie found herself in the position of long-term caregiver. As he slowly recovered, he wouldn't keep his hands off her. He called sex his "morphine." She told us caregiving changed the way she saw him. No longer an active partner, he became more like a patient. Only in her early fifties, Julie felt old, drained of energy, pulling away from him, even though she loved him dearly. When he regained health, her libido still registered zero.

2. *J*ulie wanted to desire her husband as in the past, but felt stuck as a nurse with a patient. Recount a time when your husband's health issues adversely affected your libido. _____

_____

_____

_____

3. *W*hat gentle words could Julie use to delay a sexual encounter for a better time? _____

_____

_____

_____

4. *W*hat would you say to Julie to encourage her? _____

_____

_____

_____

Stella

Stella sat near the door as if strategically positioned for a quick getaway. Toward the end of the sessions, when she finally reached out to the group, we learned that in their early sixties both she and Herb had gained significant weight. He drank more heavily than in the past and began to have difficulty finishing sex (ejaculating). When she found he returned to an old pornography habit, Stella wondered if porn use, weight-gain, and increased alcohol intake might be related to his sexual issue. If so, what could she do? She certainly couldn't fix his problems. Stella also defended her practice of faking orgasms. Many of these issues will be tackled in this chapter, but as you consider Stella and Herb…

5. ...What do you think are their most serious problems? _____

_____

_____

_____

6. What health issues may be inadvertently affecting your love life? _____

_____

_____

_____

Read on to discover how we can help our husbands at such a time as this.

Men's Emotional Sexual Enemies

Joel 2:25
"I will restore the years the locust has eaten."

Our patio conversation continued. As he sipped coffee his chest heaved in a long sigh. "I can't help but look at how time has just gone. I was gonna be this and do that... but here I am, staring at seventy, and nothing much to show for my life... it feels like failure."

Now I spoke up. "You aren't a failure, Honey. You have accomplished a great deal. Look at your amazing family, all these grands... leadership of the men's luncheon, your constant work on this beautiful home!" I didn't even have to think... the words just came. I so wanted to fix this!

He shook his head. "You aren't really hearing me, Babe. I can't go back. I can't get those lost years. I fight this feeling more and more the older I get."

The aging process packs an emotional as well as physical wallop to your man. The more you know about his struggles, the more you can help him. You can't restore the years he's lost – only God can give him the sense of recovered time. But besides the time we all lose each second, what *has* your husband lost?

Confidence.

He hates to admit it. Whether spoken out loud in a moment of transparency, or guarded carefully within his heart, the dread of aging can batter his masculine soul. As your man grapples with these thoughts, he may also feel like a failure in the bedroom.

All the emotional issues below steal his confidence every bit as much as physical ones do. Respond to each question with a heart of compassion to walk in his shoes.

Depression

Depression from a death, sudden disappointment, or heredity can disrupt a husband's sexual function. Even mild depression can put a speed bump in his libido. If your husband is sad, don't expect sex to be amazing, and allow time to do some detective work. What might have triggered a downturn? Depression can run in families. Are you aware of this in your husband's family of origin? Do you see him spiralling down during certain times of the year?

1. If you see a pattern of depression, write about it here. _____

_____

_____

_____

Pressure at Work

Pressure at work or loss of a job will cause a man to want/need the comfort of warm relaxing sex, quickie sex, or no sex at all. Bereft of emotional energy, he wants distraction or solitude to decompress. Though men may be built for work pressure, an overload can rob you of a great lover.

On a slightly different note, workaholism can also affect a man's sex drive. Men stay at work for many reasons – too much to get done in a normal day, trouble at home, pressure from bosses, or a need for the kudos of early arrival or staying late. Sometimes he is most fulfilled through his job. If your husband is a workaholic, search out the reason and talk about how it impacts your relationship.

2. *D*o you recall a time your husband struggled sexually because of trouble at work? How did you deal with it? How did you keep discouragement at bay while waiting for the crisis to pass? _____

_____

_____

_____

_____

Bitterness, Irritability, Boredom, and Shame

That's a lot to put on one line. The first three are symptoms, the last one is a cause. Some homes suffer under the weight of frustration and anger. Negativity can come from both sides, but sometimes even with a cheerful wife, a husband may find little things to complain or vent about. These behaviors indicate deeper issues and certainly steal joy from the bedroom.

Like termites eating away at the foundation of a house, disappointment or trauma destroy from the inside out. One husband dealt with the termites of shame from a rejecting father. Another's foundation crumbled from past raucous drug-dealing and casual sex.

Though I fell in love with my husband as an enthusiastic new Christian, our marriage soon trembled above our shaky emotional foundation. His early first marriage left him emotionally shattered. For a long time I felt it must be me, but slowly I learned that when he seemed most distant or irritable, he was fighting a silent war with shame.

No one escapes the effects of shame. The accusations of our enemy combine with our own self-condemnation to wreak havoc on relationships. My guy now realizes that freedom comes only in fully receiving Christ's blood-bought forgiveness – and forgiving himself. Does your man know how much God loves him?

Long-lasting sweetness in a relationship is a byproduct of contentment within. A better sex life emerges from the rubble. Have you ever seen bitterness and irritability turn a husband (or a wife, or both) into a porcupine, making the other want to stay clear of those spines? Most of us have.

3. Do you see your husband's sense of failure and/or painful memories disconnecting him from you? What did you (will you) do to alleviate his pain?

_____

_____

_____

_____

Other Stress

One husband, normally a kind and skilled lover, began to finish sex within three or four minutes. After several weeks, the wife asked why. He said he felt terrible about it but didn't know. Together, they pieced together the problem. They had recently taken in a pregnant teenager whose baby they planned to adopt. Though she hadn't caused any problems in the home and was actually a pleasant guest, he felt stressed. So much so that he altered his normal sexual procedure.

Any stresses in your guy's life will likely show up in the bedroom. Your calm detective work and proactive engagement can help put him back on track.

4. Do you recall a time when your husband changed his normal sexual patterns? How did you discover the reason, and how did the problem work out over time? _____

_____

_____

_____

_____

Pornography

Have you ever talked to your husband about pornography? To your teenagers? This conversation, though terribly difficult, must happen. And it's no longer just a male issue. Women are becoming addicted to pornography as well.

Since men usually begin the habit in their single years, even as pre-teens, they wrongly think getting married will satisfy their need. It never does, because pornography uses different neural pathways in the brain. They get hooked on a series of changing images, even when they know their wives are right there, available. To keep the dopamine and other drugs flooding their brains, they constantly revert back to the screen. When pornography becomes a compulsion, an addiction, shame sets up shop and hunkers down for the long haul. Even as our society defends the whole sex industry, it reels under the drastic consequences. Families are devastated. Husbands hide.

Besides the temptation to seek thrills in new, different women in affairs, a man may no longer find pleasure in his wife's body. If she doesn't arouse him as images do, he may stop having sex with her altogether. When his brain rewires to respond to screens rather than a person, sex devoid of smell, taste, and imperfection can seem easier. It requires no relational component. Men who once thought sex with a live human female would be heaven on earth now become bored with *normal*. Only *different* will do the trick. Our society hasn't yet come to grips with the physiological and relational carnage of this sexual *cheat*.

How serious is the porn habit in men past fifty? Serious. Pornography is just too easy. One click and you're there. Older men took risks in buying porn in their youth. New addictions start every minute. Add to that, the urologists who encourage older patients to use pornography to "get back on your feet" after prostate cancer.

What can we do to stop the continuing ravages of porn use in our families? With appropriate help from a counselor, or a program like "Conquer," (an online course),[1] or the accountability of the excellent "Covenant Eyes," (computer application),[2] men can break free of the bondage and shame. Your marriage can have a fresh start with loving, yet firm accountability.

5. *How* has pornography affected your marriage? You? Your husband? How will you broach the topic for a conversation? _____

_____

_____

_____

_____

_____

6. As you and your husband face health challenges ahead, remember the comforting verses in Romans 8 which remind us that even when we don't know how to pray, the Holy Spirit prays for us "according to God's will." That's the kind of prayer I need. Talk to the Lord in a simple prayer about your husband's emotional needs. Sometimes a good way to start is simply, "Lord, please help!"

_____

_____

_____

_____

_____

_____

Men's Physical Sexual Enemies

*H*ow much does your husband's sexual function matter to him? A lot! As his chosen partner for life, minimizing its importance won't help him. You may want to say, "Oh, Honey. There's more to us than that!" Though it's true, get into *his* head. Realize *his* thoughts about *his* sexuality make the difference between a happy life and an unnecessarily sad one.

The three most common thieves of men's sexual satisfaction are: 1) an insufficient erection, 2) an erection which doesn't last long enough to ejaculate during sex, and 3) little or no interest in sex – low libido. The emotional fallout from these symptoms runs the gamut from concerned annoyance to a serious sense of failing manhood.

Let's talk about the third one first – low libido. If this intruder has encroached on your love life, take action by making a urology appointment to determine his testosterone levels. "Low T," or low testosterone, doesn't necessarily affect all erectile dysfunction (ED), but if his levels are low, below 300 (average ranges 350-800), prescribed creams, under-skin pellets, or injections of testosterone may help. My OB-GYN says testosterone therapy improves only about 50% of low libido cases. That's because stress and other factors contribute to the problem.

Is low libido an issue for your husband? Ask him how he views his situation and really listen when he talks. Encourage him with your upbeat attitude. Even more importantly, touch him more than ever. Tell him you find him handsome and desirable. Be available for lounging around, relaxing together.

In our next section, we will discuss TRT, testosterone replacement therapy, in greater detail.

Your husband *can* overcome his libido difficulties. Cliff and Joyce Penner are Christian sex therapists who've written many books. You can find a few on our AWE Book List. Good reading material and encouraging words may open the door to important discussions. As you talk about the physical causes of sexual dysfunction, tread softly. You may find some of the culprits surprising.

Extra Weight

Over 75% of us tend to gain weight after fifty. For men, too much extra weight hinders their sex drive, energy, and ability to perform sexually. If your guy has trouble with either sex or the buffet bar, talk to him about the difference twenty or thirty pounds could make in your love life.

1. *W*rite how you might start the conversation and practice it a few times.

_____

_____

_____

_____

Sugar/Carbs

You may have thought the topic of weight covered the problem of sugar and carbs. Not quite. It's probable that even when a thin man chows down on a carb-loaded pizza or pint of ice cream at 10:00 p.m., he most likely won't be *in the mood* at 11:00 p.m. − no matter how thin he is. A person high on carbs doesn't do his sex life any favors. He'll probably fall asleep in twelve seconds or less, wake up at six, and desire what he missed the night before. Carbohydrates like bread and pastas turn into sugar during digestion.

They steal both stamina and disease-fighting properties of the body. While okay in moderation, they're definitely best earlier in the day.

2. *H*ow might you convince your man to eat dessert closer to 7:00 than midnight? _____

_____

_____

_____

Many Medications

Men take the following meds for years not realizing the effect they may have on their sex life. Often, there's no choice, but losing weight or making a few lifestyle adjustments may remove the need for some of these medications. Which ones take up residence in your medicine cabinet?

_____ Blood pressure medications

_____ Reflux meds like Nexium or Omeprazole

_____ Antidepressants/anti-anxiety medications

_____ Anti-inflammatory pain meds (such as Ibuprofen)

_____ Heavy-duty pain meds (like hydrocodone)

_____ A few more: Tagamet, Dramamine, Benadryl, Phenergan, Zantac

Alcohol

I read a T-shirt at the beach which shared enlightening information: "Beer has been helping people have sex for over 200 years." Though not a history buff, I suspect beer has helped people have sex way longer than that. But did it help them have good sex? Alcohol, a depressant, promotes relaxation. It gives a guy some confidence, maybe, to make a sexual move, but it's real effect causes the experience to be less intense. In a word, alcohol is counterproductive to good sex. As men grow older, larger intake may even hinder their ability to complete sex.

3. $\mathcal{H}$ow has alcohol played a part in your sex life? _____

_____

_____

_____

Lack of Exercise

Men tend to become more sedentary as they age. The inevitable aches and pains from a desk job, or the stress of an outdoor job, may make exercise difficult to start. Procrastination makes it harder. Encourage your guy to find a weekly basketball game or a daily gym workout to rev up his sexual function.

How does exercise work to improve our sex lives? It produces feel-good hormones – boosts testosterone – and helps the heart and lungs function better. It promotes good circulation throughout the body's lymph system. Exercise and sex create a circle of energy. The more we engage in both, the more we enjoy sex. Note our small disclaimer alert: While exercise increases a desire for sex, sex may not increase a desire for exercise.

4. $\mathcal{H}$ow can you open this conversation so your man will see the connection between exercise and libido? Could you exercise together? _____

_____

_____

_____

_____

Sickness, Injury, Sexless Months

Men's interest in sex sometimes defies explanation. Why in the middle of the night? Why while I'm painting the den? Why at five a.m.? But it gets worse. Men can spike a 102 degree fever and ask for sex along with a glass of water. A friend's husband asked for sex right after being released from the hospital after brain surgery. Another friend's husband had bandaged forearms with second degree burns but wanted sex as soon as he got home from the E.R. It's true. Men's libido can survive a lot of physical stress.

Husbands get frustrated missing sex for a week or two. Wives, on the other hand, generally grow less interested after a while without lovemaking. However, our reaction to abstinence *reverses* after several months. We women eventually miss the *emotional connection* – and long for it again. But what about the husband after a year without sex? He is more likely to accept a new normal. His body adjusts.

Abstinence demonstrates men's and women's general motivations for engaging sexually. For the majority of men, sex is primarily physical, secondarily emotional. Once the physical need wears off, the emotional need may not click in.

So, men can be radically affected *negatively* by long-term illness or injury. After several months or a year, he may retreat into sexual hermit mode. The wife hurts, but he does too. He needs her more than he realizes.

5. *Tell* of a time when sex was tabled due to a sickness, injury, or pain like arthritis? How did you handle the abstinence?_____

_____

_____

_____

Hearing Loss

Wife: Are you listening to me? Did you hear a word I said?

Husband: No, I didn't hear you. Say it again.

Wife: Really? Repeat the whole thing?

Husband: You were mumbling!

After discussions about hearing loss with men and their wives while writing this book, the problem seems prevalent enough to require its own space. Of all the daily, incessant issues a man eventually faces, this one ranks high. When he starts to lose his hearing, he also begins to dread parties, church events, restaurants, and family gatherings. Mere talk on the phone becomes a chore. With only one or two in a quiet conversation, your husband seems content. But talking with three or more people in a public space, he wilts.

Does this affect him sexually? I can give you at least three ways. You may be able to add more.

a. The two of you quarrel because he doesn't want to attend an event. The joy in your relationship erodes because he feels you don't understand him. He initiates sex less. You initiate less. He feels rejected as well as falling apart.

b. He begins to feel paranoid. When everyone else laughs at the joke he didn't hear, or they don't quite hear him because his hearing problem makes him quieter, he begins to withdraw. Thinking he is different and clueless in social situations, he feels different even from you. He loses his sense of manliness.

c. When his hearing loss gets to the point where he needs to go through the excruciating process of finding the right hearing aids, he feels old. He feels he is past his vigor. Hearing aids are permanent, not like crutches. He feels too old to pursue sex like he used to.

6. If hearing loss has stolen joy from your home, tell how you've dealt with it. How can you encourage your husband to see this has nothing whatsoever to do with his desirability to you? _____

_____

_____

_____

Prostate Cancer

Sometime during a man's life, the prostate gland, through which the urethra travels to the penis, may become enlarged, causing more trips to the bathroom. Some studies indicate that a regular sex life *may* keep the prostate healthy. However, cancer refuses to fit into any box. It strikes when least expected. When prostate cancer attacks a younger man, he faces a serious, life-threatening situation; but the disease responds well to treatment in men over fifty.

After a biopsy of the gland shows cancer cells, treatment may call for the removal of the prostate, sometimes followed by radiation therapy. Since surgery can easily nick vital nerves needed for sexual function, no man wants to receive this directive.

Often, radiation alone stops the cancer. But radiation doesn't provide a much better prospect for sex. Radiation leaks into surrounding tissue, eventually causing damage to nerves over the course of two to ten years. No wonder so much fear and apprehension surrounds this gland. Hopefully, the basic information you find here will help you and your man feel more at ease.

By age ninety, 90% of men will have prostate cancer on some level of severity. All men should be screened by age fifty; those with a family history should go earlier. The PSA count (a blood test) shows whether a prostate biopsy is necessary. That dreaded rectal digital exam, the gloved finger which keeps men away from the doctor, can reveal an enlarged prostate. Make sure your husband doesn't avoid his duty to both you and himself!

I fervently hope and pray that women gathered together in AWE groups, Bible study classes, and cozy cafes will share their knowledge and experiences so the debilitating fear surrounding this subject will lose its power. You already know why I'm so passionate about this. My husband's diagnosis in 2014 *did* cause our sex life to falter for a time. Thankfully, God, through his grace and our persistence, led us to solutions which revved us up again. Never let prostate cancer survivors or their families tell you this diagnosis pronounces the death sentence to a good sex life. It isn't true.

The following *is* true:

A decade before his cancer diagnosis, over dinner, my husband told me of a customer he met on the job. The man shared that his wife had just divorced him because of prostate cancer. "I'm no good to her anymore… that's what she said, anyway… I guess I'm no good to any woman now."

When my husband told me this story, I asked, "Was the man under eighty years old?"

"Yes, he seemed to be in his early fifties," he said.

"Well," I went on, "can he work?"

"Sure."

"Honey, that man can be plenty good to a woman! He has everything he needs – hands, lips, and a beating heart. His wife was wrong. She must have wanted an excuse to leave."

Little did I know God would one day require me to make good on my declaration. From that day on, I wondered how many men believed prostate cancer steals their sex lives. Now I stand on a personal soapbox. We will cover the topic more in our next section, so read on.

7. *H*as prostate cancer shown up in your family? Write about friends, relatives, or your own experiences. In one sentence tell what you will say to your husband if you ever receive the news of this cancer. Make it a good one.____

_____

_____

_____

_____

_____

_____

_____

Men's Sexual Allies

You are your husband's greatest sexual ally. If you don't have any issues in this area now, you might think the practical help here isn't needed. Just remember, eventually your warmth and encouragement won't be enough. You will likely need this information.

Keep in mind that ED or low libido strikes younger men more and more. Virile men as young as mid-twenties have reported low sperm count, low drive, and low testosterone. As a matter of fact, average testosterone levels in males has reduced by 20% in the last two decades. Why? Our lifestyles and diet, including injection of animals with growth hormones, may have contributed to the feminization of males in our society. This should be of huge concern.

But, without succumbing to worry now, you can be armed with knowledge to help your guy in the future – if a need arises.

First let's talk about testosterone replacement therapy or TRT. Excelmale.com is a good website for more information, but for our purposes, we'll look at common symptoms of low testosterone and benefits of TRT.

Do you or your husband notice any of the following issues: mental fog, indecisiveness or hesitancy, lack of energy or work performance, decreased sex drive or ability to ejaculate, decrease in strength or endurance, or noticeable changes in behavior? If your husband struggles with four or more of the above symptoms, a simple blood test will indicate if his levels are in the normal range. TRT treatment protocols take the form of weekly intramuscular injections (a cheaper method) or transdermal cream applied to the scrotum each morning.

TRT usually has the following positive results: Improved mood, improved libido, reduced cholesterol, improved cognition, muscle mass, bone density, and general well-being. You should also see reduced fatigue and irritability.

As important as testosterone is, we've seen that libido issues are more complicated than a blood test. So, TRT may not impact libido greatly. Injections or creams may be combined with lifestyle changes (already discussed) to impact a man's sexual desire.

Now, meet my friends, Jane and Bill.

Jane, Bill, and Little Blue Pills

Jane and Bill enjoyed what most would call a passionate relationship despite some serious setbacks in the early years. In the second decade of marriage, they began to wonder if children were ever going to arrive but stopped short of any intervention. When twin boys arrived just before their fifteenth anniversary, they became Jane and Bill's all-consuming project for eighteen years.

When the twins headed off to college, Jane and Bill renewed their passion with fresh intentionality and some giddyness. One night after they left, Bill shook his head and sighed, "Whew! Just in time! I was beginning to run out of steam for this parenting teen stuff." But regarding his energy, his checkups always included a blood test for testosterone levels. They always came back in the 400 to 600 range. Normal.

With a quiet house, Bill and Jane took long walks on cool evenings and even enrolled in a Latin dance class. After both boys married in the same summer, they celebrated bigtime with a luxurious cruise.

It was on the cruise ship while celebrating their wedding anniversary, when *it* happened. In the jubilation of love, Bill sexually disappointed himself. Still, his inability to complete sex with Jane that night didn't fluster either one of them.

During the following month, settled back in the normal routines of home, *it* happened a few more times. Bill now began to worry. He'd never considered using those little blue pills. When they saw the commercials on TV, he always said, "Why, you're my Viagra, Janie!"

She would lower her head and raise her eyebrows at him over her glasses, "And don't you forget it, Mistah!"

Over the next year, Bill's libido slowly declined. To be clear, they hadn't been twice-a-week lovers for quite some time. Now, at sixty-two, they scheduled lovemaking each weekend. Their efforts caused their relationship to thrive even *when things didn't work perfectly*. Jane willingly, even joyfully, became the main initiator.

When two weekends went by without *an appointment*, Jane realized Bill had begun to opt out of sex. She finally gathered up courage to ask a slightly older girlfriend out for breakfast. Maybe she'd have some insight.

"Bill and I get along great!" Jane said. "Our sex life has been fairly smooth, especially since we started to plan ahead for our special times... but you know, he's too young to have these problems!"

Turns out Jane asked the right friend. Turns out her friend and husband had recently asked their doctor about this very issue! He encouraged them to try a blue pill to see if it worked. And it did.

That afternoon, Jane did her homework. She gathered the following information from a reputable online pharmacy.

1. Viagra, Cialis, and Levitra all have a similar active ingredient – a drug which relaxes the blood vessels in the area of the sexual organs. This causes the penis, when aroused, to be fully supplied with blood. Fully-open blood vessels sometimes increase a man's girth and length.

2. These medicines are not aphrodisiacs, so a man will **not have an erection simply by taking them**. If a man is sexually aroused, they usually work in about an hour – but *only* if he is sexually aroused.

3. Side effects sometimes occur – headaches, stuffy nose, facial flushing, stomach upset, etc.

4. Of the three meds, Cialis lasts the longest – up to 36 hours (as opposed to 4-6 hours for the others), giving it the name "Weekend Wonder." However, if any of the side effects show up, they also may last longer.

5. These medicines work for 60-70% of men with ED. As each med may affect any individual man differently, he should try all three before giving up. Also, he might try at least eight doses of each one before abandoning the treatment.

6. The tablets come in varying strengths and a tablet may be split. Try a half tab if your husband is sensitive to meds in general. If a smaller dosage works well enough for the problem to be solved, no need to use the full dosage. (Your local pharmacy sells easy-to-use pill splitters.)

7. Be careful to order these meds from reputable pharmacies. Many online sources supply fake or even dangerous pills.

After hearing about Jane's breakfast chat, Bill conducted his own research. He learned that after taking the pills for a while, some men get back on track and may not need to continue. One urologist put it this way, "A penis doesn't make an orgasm. The brain does. If the brain regains the confidence it once lost, successful function can often resume."

Bill never learned why he lost his ability to perform sexually. With a great wife and a good life, it didn't make any sense. He took the pills for about four months, then began to forget them sometimes. So the pills got old well before Bill did.

Here's an out-in-the-open secret: men and women rarely talk about these things to close friends – often not even to each other. Notice how Jane and Bill's brief recurring conversation during TV commercials set the standard for great sex?

Women who appreciate their sex lives might cry at times when lovemaking is stressful and even feel as though something's wrong with them. It's harder for a woman to just clam up. Thank goodness. It's a good thing if tears lead to a conversation. Yet men can let months, even years, go by before talking to his wife or a doctor. Like a low-grade fever in the home, drama may surface *around* the issue, but never *about* the issue.

Are you the Bill and Jane who live on Every Street in Everytown, USA? Do you think only single men or old guys in their eighties use these pills? Urologists stand ready to help men of *every* age with *every* concern or question about their sexual function. By age fifty, men should:

1. Get checked for low testosterone – a blood test. (Levels may be checked at any age.) Low libido or fatigue may be caused by other conditions, but at least rule out Low T.

2. Check PSA blood levels. This test can (but may not always) find prostate issues.

3. Get that uncomfortable digital exam to check for an enlarged prostate.

4. Ask for samples of the blue pills: Cialis, Levitra, and/or Viagra.

When Blue Pills Don't Work

Sometimes other methods are needed for treating ED. If you don't need the following section now, it will be waiting for you further down the road, just in case.

- A cylindrical suction chamber comes in many designs, and each one works in a slightly different way. With the penis inside the chamber which presses against the groin and abdomen, a simple pump creates a vacuum which draws blood into the penis. The resulting erection can last long enough to complete intercourse. Has the blue pill produced side effects which your husband finds unacceptable? This method may be an option. It also may work for those who have found the pill ineffective.

- Injections directly into the side of the penis can produce an erection in three minutes or less. There are several drugs which doctors prescribe for these shots, so if one doesn't work, another might. Also, the amount of medicine needed may vary from one man to another, so this is trial and error. Of course, a guy has to be okay with injecting himself in this tender spot.

- Finally, the IPP or Implanted Penile Prosthesis is the most invasive, but will **guarantee successful intercourse**.

In surgery, a new mechanical hydraulics system replaces (that's right, literally replaces) the natural one. A bulb, placed inside the scrotum, when squeezed eight to 20 times, pumps fluid from a lemon-sized reservoir (housed in the low, hollow part of the man's abdomen) into new tubes in the penis.

This device takes no batteries. It is completely mechanical and operated by learning the position of the pump and how to press the bulb which opens the valve and moves the liquid. The penis stays erect until he presses a button (a release valve) which allows the liquid to flow back into its reservoir.

The Erection That Lasts as Long as You Want sounds like a dream; and believe it or not, thousands of men undergo the difficult surgery for this "dream" every day, all day, around the world!

However, make this decision with caution. Here's more information.

a. This surgical procedure removes the possibility of creating an erection the old way. Forever. So the only erection a man will ever have again is through using the prosthesis pump. ***This is not to say men don't feel aroused in the groin area. They do.*** And it is very pleasurable. ***Orgasm is normal with this device.***

b. Recovery from the procedure isn't a piece of cake. Most men must avoid physical work for several weeks – especially while on pain meds. Also, the pump can't be used for sex for at least six weeks.

c. Once healed, the prosthesis *must* be pumped up every single day for six months, whether used for sex or not. This allows the skin to stretch and heal on the inside, preventing scar tissue from building up.

d. The small appliance hides inside the scrotum, *completely invisible*, but the couple must adjust to the feel of the mechanical addition to his anatomy.

That's a lot to take in, and you may not ever need the information for yourselves. But think about how you can help other women with information that can encourage them.

The main takeaway from this section is to remind yourself every day that your relationship is worth all the trouble the two of you expend to solve sexual issues. The closeness of this kind of bond was never meant to fade away. So don't give up when times get tough.

Finally, the following email, edited for length, will close out this chapter.

Virginia's Letter – The Secret

The Argentinian wisp of a woman, dark and wrinkled in her seventies, owned and operated a business as well as mentored her eleven adult children. In this private email to me, she discloses a secret all husbands and wives need to know.

> ...you noted, as we grow older, or get depressed by multiple problems, and take various medications with side effects not advertised, our testosterone levels go down. This (oxytocin)... is called the "hormone of desire" for both men and women... I know the man I loved so much was turned on by my enthusiasm when I saw him. I know that even when I wasn't in the mood, and responded because of my love for him, I was surprised at the sudden strength of my response. If I had not tried out of my love for him, we would have lost that moment together and the renewed bonding that followed.
>
> ...I also think a romantic moment... doesn't necessarily have to follow through to the end. Whatever you leave for the next time builds up over time and makes the (next) encounter even more

passionate. The moment is not lost, it is just put on pause while the energy keeps building up. For this reason a man should not feel under pressure to perform each time. He should take pleasure in the happiness he brings to his wife and the closeness they share – and look forward to the next time.

There are men and women who have been taught that sex is evil and once the strong drive of youth has diminished and the need to reproduce is past, it is no longer justified. This is a mistake. Sexual communication, as you observed, is still very important to bonding and overall health and enthusiasm for life. A man I once knew said, "If we insult sex, we insult God, for he made this way for men and women to become one. Sex can be just as good or bad as we make it. It is up to us to achieve the potential that God envisioned when he gave us this gift of love..."

Sincerely, Virginia

8

A Time to Light the Fire

The Song of Solomon –
A Rhapsody of Love

Song of Solomon 8:7
"Many waters cannot quench love, neither can floods drown it. If a man offered for love all the wealth of his house, he would be utterly despised."

Tucked in the middle of our Bible is a poem/song/play which Jewish rabbis used to teach young men about God's view of marital love. Attributed to Solomon as author, this small book packs a huge message about marriage. It not only extols the glories of romantic and sexual love, it most importantly illuminates God's deep love for his bride, Israel, and now us, his church. It acknowledges common difficulties in the marriage relationship, and it's very steamy!

The story features three main characters: a young woman called the Shulammite (we'll call her Shula), a young man (possibly Solomon himself), and a chorus of narrators who vocalize the thoughts of God. Bible scholars agree the play presents an allegory comparing God's love to the love of a bridegroom. But thousands of generations have stood in awesome amazement at this bride's passionate response! God not only approves of the sexuality he created for both husband and wife – he celebrates it!

146

On the intricate meanings of the text, however, scholars' agreement ends. Does the poem depict actual events – or is it a fictional couple? What role did Solomon play in the story? Was he both author and central lover, possibly disguised as a shepherd boy? Or did he ride into the countryside in all his splendor to woo a girl? Or might he be the author, at home in his palace, envisioning a rural couple with whom he can barely relate?

The dilemma of Solomon's role springs from what the Bible tells us about his hundreds of wives and concubines. In I Kings 11:4 scripture says, *"For when Solomon was old, his wives turned away his heart after other gods, and his heart was not wholly true to the Lord his God, as was the heart of David his father."* Your Bible notes may give more insight, but because of his real-life kingship, we lean towards viewing Solomon as a scribe of the Lord rather than Shula's actual husband.

Can you picture Solomon's hands trembling as he tries to hold his quill steady? It might have been tough writing on parchment these profound, inspired, dictated thoughts about the most valued reality this side of heaven. God gave him wisdom, wealth, and power. In this book you will find out what trumps all.

Before embarking on this journey, however, read the text in its entirety. This can probably be accomplished in less than an hour. View this story as God's magnificent love-making manual. Then come back to the study and allow God to continue his work in your heart and marriage.

Song of Solomon – Chapter 1 – Flirting

1. Song of Solomon 1: 2 The theme of the book is set. Remember the jump rope jingle? *You and your fella sittin' in a tree, K-i-s-s-i-n-g.* The couple here may not be kissing yet, but they want to. They run and daydream. She compares her guy to a king bringing her into his chambers. How does the girl describe herself in real life in verses 5 and 6? What might she mean by "my own vineyard"?

_____

_____

_____

2. In Chapter 1:7-8, the girl flirts but does not want to be like "a veiled woman." What does she mean, and how does the couple plan to meet regularly, appropriately, in public? _____

_____

_____

_____

3. This chapter ends with the couple back in reality. As they grow deeper in love, they compliment each other. Describe their actual place of courtship (1:16, 17). Not a palace, much of the action in this poem takes place outdoors. What can we learn for our own marriage spice-up? Will you get outside to enjoy each other soon? Copy two favorite phrases from these romantic verses.

_____

_____

_____

_____

_____

Chapter 2 – Longing

1. The lovers must deal with being "in love" in public, something frowned upon in those days. In Chapter 2:2-3, they compare each other to the others they might have chosen. Do you look for ways to see your lover shine above other men? Share the phrases of comparison and choose which ones you can use to compliment your man. _____

_____

_____

_____

_____

2. On Chapter 2:4-6, Shula describes the wait for her wedding day and tells us she is sick with love. However, she educates herself about lovemaking through her imagination. She has allowed **attraction** to move to the next step, **arousal**, in her mind. Our first instruction about foreplay comes in verse 6 and *is repeated* later in the Song. Write it here and speculate what it means that "his right hand embraces me." _____

_____

_____

_____

_____

3. Shula addresses the chorus in verse 7, "O daughters of Jerusalem," with the first of three identical warnings about love. Copy that warning here._____

_____

_____

_____

4. On verses 8-14, Shula expresses her thoughts about enjoying each other again in a beautiful outdoor setting. In verse 10, she invites him to *come away*. Begin here to use colored pencils to circle references to the five senses in relating to each other. Our senses are our tools for making love: sight, taste, smell, touch, hearing. Choose a color for each sense, and as you circle phrases, see the rainbow in your Bible. We used the following: purple=sight, red=touch, orange=taste, blue=hearing, green=smell.

Write how many of each sense you found. _____

_____

_____

_____

_____

5. What might verse 15 mean in reference to "the little foxes"? This couple is aware of what could come between them. How can you relate in your own relationship? _____

_____

_____

_____

Chapter 3 – Dreaming

1. Our Shula dreams she loses her lover and finds him out in the streets (3:1-4). In verse 5, she again warns the other girls "not to stir up love until…" We see fears of abandonment, needing of help, and a strong desire to secure her love. How can you relate to the fears or other emotions expressed in this dream?

_____

_____

_____

_____

_____

2. Shula, in 3:6-11, also imagines her lover arriving at the wedding as the king with his royal caravan. Can you share a part of your own wedding which makes this daydream understandable? _____

_____

_____

_____

_____

Chapter 4 – The Marriage Consummation

1. In Chapter 4:1-11, the shepherd lover admires his new wife's body, at first, mostly by sight. Notice a pattern for our foreplay? Do you want to share your beauty with your husband? Like this shepherd, he wants to see every detail. To what objects in nature and court does this lover compare his wife's body? Might she be wearing some jewelry? _____

_____

_____

_____

_____

_____

2. Notice in 4:12-16 that passion has come to its fullest. The husband now approaches his wife's "locked garden." To what do you think that locked garden refers? _____

_____

_____

3. We assume this garden has been locked to him until now, at marriage. What a momentous occasion! Her aroma is close enough to fully experience, and her arousal is indicated by the first mention of "fountains." What might her *fountains* be? _____

_____

_____

4. As you read the final verse in the chapter, to what do you think it might refer? _____

_____

_____

Chapters 5, 6, 7 – The Honeymoon

1. "*E*at, friends, drink, and be drunk with love!" These words, spoken by our loving Father, refer to the afterglow of lovemaking. Then, in verses 2-8, the bride dreams again, this time in the form of a terrible nightmare consisting of two parts. Describe the first part of the dream (v. 2-5). _____

_____

_____

_____

2. *F*rom v. 6-8, we see a sexually awake woman. If she thought she was love-sick before, her "affliction" is worse now. What happens in the second part of her dream? _____

_____

_____

_____

3. *D*escribe a time early in your marriage when your intense love brought insecurities?_____

_____

_____

_____

4. *I*n Chapter 5:10-16, the bride now admires her husband's body. Notice how she sees him in terms of strength and tenderness at the same time? Trust has built and made her more open about the physical part of her passion. Quote her words referring to his strength and her words of his tenderness. Strength – _____

_____

Tenderness –_____

_____

5. As you ponder the statement above, do you recognize your husband's desire for you? How will you show your appreciation for his desire this week?

_____

_____

_____

_____

_____

In Chapter 6, after the bride refers to her husband's constant attention to her "garden of spices," she speaks of ownership of each other. "I am my beloved's and my beloved is mine." These are great words of trust. We see the words again in 7:10. Here she ups the ante. "I am my beloved's and his desire is for me." Can you see how their lovemaking is a symbol, an intensely pleasurable symbol, of their exclusive bond with each other? God wants couples to bond in this way because he designed the marriage to form a secure foundation for generations.

6. Ponder this passage in light of love growing stronger as years go by. Is this happening in your marriage? It has been said that if our love isn't going forward, it is slipping backward. What will you do to grow the sweetness in your relationship?_____

_____

_____

_____

_____

_____

Notice in Chapter 6:4-9, the husband praises his wife in a broader way. Besides repeating some of her physical attributes from other passages, he says she is more beautiful than all of Solomon's harem (v. 8, 9). Then in verse 10, his rapture elevates her to a heavenly being. This statement shows that he thinks more of her as his wife than when they first fell in love. What a thrilling pattern! Your husband likely feels the same way towards you.

7. In Chapter 7, as he continues to praise the bride's beauty, he says what he will do to her. Find the verse where he describes a lovemaking action with the word, "will". What will you do to engage in lovemaking from a position of *doing the loving thing* rather than doing what comes naturally? _____

_____

_____

8. The chapter ends with another invitation to enjoy the outdoors. This time they are married and will really camp. Her mention of mandrakes refers to their aphrodisiac qualities. Obviously, she wants this trip to be for lovemaking.

Couples need getaways – times which create memories to cherish for the rest of their lives. Plan a three to five-day getaway this year. Where will you go? This couple didn't go far. You don't have to either. Just far enough to be AWAY.

_____

_____

Chapter 8 – The Epilogue

The Song of Solomon ends with high praise for marital love. Once again, the bride longs to be openly affectionate in public. She warns the young daughters of Jerusalem for the third time not to stir up or awaken love until it pleases. In 8:6-7, we see a positive use of the word "jealousy." God is jealous for our love. No other love is to come between us and Him. Listen to the words of high emotion! The grave, fire, floods, wealth – none of these can drown out the song of love!

In the finale, we see a hint of chagrin at the wealth of Solomon. All of his vine-dressers, all of his grapes, all of his vineyards mean nothing – for no worldly treasure compares to love. Love is not a commodity. I can't help but wonder what Solomon felt and thought as these words flowed from his pen to the parchment in front of him.

In a closing word of invitation, the wife invites her husband to make love to her. Nowhere in this song do we see love lose its grip on the hearts of this couple. God allows life to go on with all its troubles and woe, for that is the context in which we learn to trust Him and to love others the way He loves us. Children and health and wealth may come and go, but one constant remains. Love.

1. *C*opy your three favorite verses from the song here. Memorize one to keep with you. _____

_____

_____

2. *W*rite a prayer using one of the verses you chose. Refer to your husband by name and use several other phrases from the Song. Below is an example to get you started. _____

_____

_____

Dear Father,

Help me to look at my sweet husband with these words in my heart and mind, that "his mouth is most sweet," that he is "altogether desirable" (5:16). Help me to see him as "my beloved and my friend" every day!

In Jesus' Name, Amen.

9

A Time to Negotiate

Five Secrets of Sexual Fulfillment

Song of Solomon 8:3
"His left hand is under my head, and his right hand embraces me."

I pulled into the driveway listening to a rather strange conversation on talk radio. *Now, what did the host say?* I turned off the engine and listened.

"Seems to me, the ultimate sexual experience for women is a gene. Most have it, but my wife doesn't."

Seriously? On the radio? Immediately a male caller reacted. "Just want you to know," said he, "there's no such gene. But, your wife might be having trouble because of the person she's sexually involved with." Ouch. Though the comment hit the radio host rather personally, I was glad I didn't have to make the enlightening call. The audience needed to hear loud and clear: his wife was not missing a gene.

No secret, right? Yet, with all the supposed enlightenment of this modern age, there's no shortage of misconceptions regarding sex. Add a mentality of entitlement to privacy which practically encourages deceit and no one really knows what people are doing. They just assume they know. Beyond a general agreement that the sexes function somewhat differently when it comes to orgasm, false information abounds.

158

Though God designed sex as a pleasure-filled union for married people, falling in love and getting married often fail to release women's full range of sexual delights. It's time to let the secrets out! You and I weren't the only ones who had a difficult honeymoon. Oftentimes, months or *years* pass before a wife can relax and enjoy lovemaking as God designed it. Interviews with thousands of married women revealed that most don't reach their peak of sexual fulfillment until between the twelfth and fifteenth year of marriage. If you are past those anniversaries, you aren't alone, either.

You are in the right place to grow in your understanding of orgasm. Possibly you believe:

- Real (or best) orgasms happen *during* intercourse.
- Women have orgasms only if they are completely *in love*.
- Sexual Intercourse defines sex. Other sexual activities aren't actually sex.

Each of the above statements is false. Any act of sexual (genital) arousal through various kinds of touch, including but not limited to sexual intercourse, is sex. Hopefully, the following Five Secrets of Sexual Fulfillment will answer some important questions for you.

1st Secret: Relaxed Patience is Key to Fulfillment

Some women wonder if they've had an orgasm. They feel a rush of excitement before the husband ejaculates, but after he does, a feeling of sadness follows. If this is you, though your experience isn't uncommon, you can be assured the experience of climax will leave you fulfilled, not frustrated. Let's look at the verse heading this section.

His left hand is under my head, and his right hand embraces me.
Song of Solomon 8:3

God gives us this brief tip on arousal in his Sex 101 textbook, Song of Solomon, not once but three times! When God repeats concepts, we'd better listen because he's telling us something important. In this verse, a sweet moment of lovemaking shows the husband caressing (translated *embrace*) his wife with his right hand while cradling her head and body in the circle of his left arm. In this position she can lie on her back and build arousal in her own time. How beautiful.

A Time to Negotiate

We learned in Chapter 6 that **Attraction**, **Arousal**, and **Orgasm** function as three separate brain functions. Each one can stand alone. Let's look at two cases which illustrate the separation of brain functions. First, how can climax occur separately from arousal? You may have a friend who woke up from a deep sleep in the middle of an orgasm. It doesn't happen to all women, but it happens — sometimes with no memory of any sexual dream.

Secondly, you may also wonder how arousal is possible without the introductory feelings of desire or attraction. The strange truth about women is they often don't get into the mood for sex until they are in the middle of it. In this case, arousal skips right over desire or attraction.

Some sex experts divide the lovemaking experience into five parts, **Attraction**, **Arousal**, **Plateau**, **Orgasm**, and **Resolution**. The first two parts, Attraction and Arousal, can be illustrated by a train heading up the tracks on a hill. The train leaves the station with *attraction*, then moves up the hill focused on building enjoyable tension — blood congestion in the genitals.

So much happens in the brain during this climb, the commitment of marriage provides not only a greater sense of security, but also the time, safety, and comfort needed to learn about our bodies. We *choose* to become aroused by focusing on pleasure. That means thoughts of the kids and groceries have to go.

The Plateau, actually part of arousal in the brain, describes a critical moment when at the top of the hill, the height of arousal, there may be a *slight sense of leveling out*. Will the train go over the top to climax, or will it fall backward? We have to continue that stimulation or touch or movement for a few more seconds. When we crest the hill, blood rushes out from its dense congestion, causing the flood of delightful pleasure, the climax.

How do we get over the top? Sometimes you need more oxygen and must be aware to breathe. Or holding your breath while keeping the abdomen tight may work better. Patience, and joyful *presence* get you there. Don't rush or push yourself. It will sabotage the journey.

Female orgasms aren't created equal. Sometimes a climax will last a few short seconds with a tranquil feeling of being satisfied; other times the pleasure rolls in waves for almost a full minute and leaves us exquisitely exhausted. Sometimes an orgasm may last a few seconds, die down, and then lead to another – or several more. With all that possibility spread out like a gourmet picnic on a checkered blanket, do you think rating orgasms for intensity is a good idea?

1. Are you tempted to be a sexual athlete? How might evaluating or grading an orgasm become a trap? _____

_____

_____

_____

Once learned, orgasm for the wife becomes the glorious exclamation point on marital intimacy. Still, no matter how proficient, the experience can evade from time to time. We are infinitely complex, so we will discuss more female intricacies later.

In the **Resolution** phase of sex, men usually fall asleep, though not all do. And most women find the experience extremely relaxing. The *afterglow* of orgasm, though definitely not better, is thought to be a wonderful part. We all would do well to stop, rest, and indulge in the sweet time of bonding which follows. Oxytocin floods the bodies of both husband and wife so they feel a tenderness upon which they can build a deeper union.

Whether we sleep afterwards or move on to the next thing, women's arc of coming down from climax is generally longer than men's. It could take from thirty minutes up to a day or more for a woman to level out. What a glorious night of deep sleep! What a refreshing morning looking into the face of the man who brought you to such heights! What energy to face the day with your whole being refreshed!

2nd Secret: Feminine Comfort, Masculine Control

Lisa silently fumed at her husband for days because it didn't seem to bother him – or he didn't pick up the clue – that she hadn't finished sex on an occasion that needed extra time. She resisted the temptation to think he didn't really care about her, but she didn't want to make a big deal out of it for fear he'd feel like a failure and emotionally move away. Of course, he'd never go anywhere; why so upset? Her frustration embarrassed her.

Frustration on various levels kicks in when our sexual *train rolls backward down the hill too close to climax*. Built-up blood congestion doesn't subside quickly, and the physical and emotional backlash can easily start a cycle of worry. *What if it happens again? What if I can't ever be that fulfilled woman? What if he doesn't get me?* Here's where the principle of Feminine Comfort/Masculine Control comes in. You might read this part to your husband.

To explain, I go back to my college years when I babysat for a nurse. On her bookshelf I found a tiny book published in the early fifties, *Sex Without Fear* by Upton and Archer.[1] It explained a foundational principle for lovemaking. The woman must be **comfortable** (no matter what position she's trying) throughout the encounter, and the man must **maintain control** of his arousal and ejaculation. Hence, *Feminine Comfort/Masculine Control*.

While a small percentage of couples regularly orgasm at the same moment, couples who spin their wheels on this desire do so needlessly. For the husband's relative ease at achieving orgasm logically dictates he provide his wife an orgasm before he ejaculates. That's where control comes in. Wives must feel free to go after pleasure during lovemaking, then enjoy his climax in her afterglow. This natural order can actually distinguish between mere sex and true lovemaking.

When we fail to climax, we can easily become discouraged. Instead, we must *choose* to anticipate the next rendezvous. Don't let a negative cycle of fear get a foothold. Tell him gently but firmly your needs. Ask for more relaxed foreplay and try the tips coming ahead.

2. *How* and when will you initiate a talk about these issues? _____

_____

_____

_____

_____

3rd Secret: Men Need and Appreciate Wife's Climax

Despite the fact that men are hardwired to find at least part of their identity in pleasing a wife, men have a learning curve, too – though a different one. *No matter how confident* a man may seem, you are his unique project for life. Just when he thinks he has you figured out sexually, he'll wake up one day and discover you've rearranged your lovemaking furniture!

This complicating factor, part of God's design, is meant to build a glorious bond between you and your husband. When the two of you must communicate for good lovemaking, you learn to be more giving, more understanding, less selfish. A wide range of sexual activities are free to married couples, so begin now to read your own personal sex manuals – each other!

Some women of every generation have said they're content without orgasm. They enjoy the sense of closeness they feel in sexual intercourse and say their husband's climax fulfills them. Several reasons may account for this attitude:

• They find some *sense of contentment* as oxytocin flows in their intimate moment.

• They have never been aroused enough to experience sexual frustration.

• They have never experienced orgasm and choose now to focus on the husband.

Men generally can't relate to this contentment. They derive immense fulfillment in bringing the same pleasure to their wife as they experience. They want to help her achieve climax either with intercourse or by another means. Creativity in producing pleasure for each other fills emotional as well as sexual needs.

3. *W*hy do you think men find the wife's climax so important? Have you asked your husband how he feels about this? What did he say?_____

_____

_____

_____

_____

_____

4. *W*ith or without the above information, some women think seeking orgasm is somehow ungodly or selfish. Where do you think these thoughts come from?

_____

_____

5. *H*ow might settling for less than God's original plan actually refute his will?

_____

_____

_____

4th Secret: Long-Term Marital Sexuality Pleases God

A post-modern attitude which pours into the mainstream through the media spouts the view that sex is best in *newness and youth*. Couples now commonly move in together as soon as they become "an item." The accumulative effect of this state of affairs reduces the pleasure of sex to something less and less special. Our society's best offering for relationship is "serial monogamy" – sexual relationships which follow one after the other – each one considered serious[2] (*Undefiled*, by Harry Schaumburg). With this *newness* belief system, aren't we in essence ripping pages out of the Bible which pertain to sex and marriage?

According to Psalm 139, our bodies, knit together in our mother's womb, delight God. Every single part, including our sex organs![3] We are fearfully and wonderfully made. Sexuality not only symbolizes his ultimate gift, intimate fellowship with him, it's also a gift in its own right.

In marriage, God's original plan for sex not only *includes* orgasm but the thrill of it becomes the capstone of his glorious design. *Even if intercourse isn't possible, he provides orgasm as an ongoing part of our marriage.* Seeking climax takes time, and many women either don't want to ask it of their husbands or take it themselves.

While lovemaking can never replace fellowship with God, we draw closer to him by crediting the Father for our sexual delights. We cherish the gift but give thanks to and worship the Giver.

Read Romans 12:1 and 1 Peter 3:1.[4] How might these verses be applied to the sexual relationship with our mate?

6. *If* a husband isn't obedient to the Word or is a clear unbeliever, how can he be won to the Lord by this kind of *conduct* from his wife? _____

_____

_____

_____

Ironically, wives whose husbands have no interest in spiritual things have reported that the sexual component of their marriage takes on much greater significance in light of their spiritual differences. Why would this be? Possibly because, whether willing to admit it or not, men can feel jealous of a God who occupies his wife's heart. He will resent the one he perceives as a threat. But when a wife makes sure her husband *knows* her love in the bedroom and in her oxytocin-filled kisses, he may be drawn to her God. In the unselfish and joyful act of lovemaking, the wife actually preaches Christ to her husband.

5th Secret: Our Enemy Hates Married Sex

Can it be true, after all we've said about the delights of marital sex, that we can get off track by pursuing sexual heights? Yes. In his attempt to thwart God's plan for marriage, Satan's world system elevates sexual indulgence beyond all restraint. In the process, marital exclusivity, safety, unity, and joy are killed.

His plan, based on the supremacy of Self, creates an idol out of *sexual function* which makes sex a vital *need* like food or water. Even Christians, lured by the promise of something better, begin to look outside the marriage for fulfillment of what they have come to believe is a right and a need.

Did you ever think of sex as a God-given right? It isn't. Nor is it a commodity to be sold in the God-wants-me-to-be-happy Marketplace. We learned in I Corinthians 6[5] that our bodies were bought with a price − Christ's blood − to house the Holy Spirit, so we choose to offer them for good works. See Romans 12:1 and 2.

Great sex, or any sex, may or may not be granted to us, just as houses, wealth, and health may not be either. Do such statements bring up angry cries of "Unfair!"? One mark of a mature person is the ability to see life as unfair in a good way. In the grand scheme of things, it isn't fair that I have a home *at all,* much less one inhabited by a husband who cares for me. Such basic blessings boggle our minds if we take a moment to ponder them. Do we focus on our blessings, or do we continually pine for more?

Surrounded by lies streaming from so many media devices, Christians may hardly notice their children growing up without a sense of sexual equilibrium. In our culture, gender is now a matter of choice. Young adults explore "other" gender options while some parents wait for their children to decide whether they want to be a girl or a boy.

When one member of our AWE class, a youth leader, gently mentioned to her group of junior high girls that God created sex, their jaws dropped in disbelief. These girls from Christian families thought of sex completely apart from God and church and grandparents. The majority of churched high schoolers and college students see no connection between sexuality, God, or marriage. Sex for them forms a necessary indicator of social and gender identity and creates emotional pain.

Do you wonder why God allows so much pain in the area of sexuality? By now, you probably see the answer lies in its importance. The problem comes from Adam's fall in the Garden of Eden and Satan's simultaneous mutiny of sexuality, not God's good design. His gift is good, but only on his tender terms.

Ask yourself if your marital frustration may indicate a misplaced emphasis on sexual function instead of oneness of heart. It's been my challenge to keep viewing sex as a privilege, not a duty expected of me, or a right to demand from my mate or God.

7. *W*hat about you? How has God's Truth answered your questions about the function of sex as opposed to heart? _____

_____

_____

_____

_____

8. After reading the Five Secrets, which one spoke most to your situation? Share it here with a brief explanation. _____

_____

_____

_____

_____

Pray, asking God to help you today where you see your greatest need.

_____

_____

_____

_____

_____

Negotiate Your Preferences

*S*amantha and Matt sometimes sit behind you at church. You've also chatted with them in the hardware store. They have happy photos on social media and you secretly wish your marriage worked as well as theirs seems to. What you don't know about them is they're completely bored in their sex life. Long ago, "anywhere, anytime, woohoo!" gave way to "same old, same old, here we go again…" Maybe you're Samantha and Matt. But, you're here because you want something better.

In AWE class one day, Samantha realized she expected her husband to know her well enough to pick up on subtle cues regarding her likes and dislikes in lovemaking. We discussed the trap of reading each other's minds and admitted it's sometimes easier than talking about some things. But mind-reading gets us nowhere, helps no one, especially in the area of lovemaking. We hesitate to come across critical and inadvertently hurt the other's feelings. Negotiating the bedroom takes courage.

Just as the young couple in the Song of Solomon *talked* about their love life, we must, too. They *shared* what they liked about each other and what they wanted to do with, to, and for each other. No matter how long we've been married, we can learn to negotiate better. As a matter of fact, discussing the how, when, and where of lovemaking becomes more important as years go by. Here are two reasons:

1. When our motivation for sex comes less from the urge of passion, almost any little thing can interfere with *the mood* or even *the idea*. The circumstances

can sometimes decide, even dictate, whether a sexual encounter will happen. Cautionary note: A Tale of Two Saturdays, page 108.

2. The sooner we learn to communicate about sexual preferences, the less awkward later. The easy way, the way of silent wishing and hoping, won't get us to the place we want to be.

Samantha's group **wondered when and where these discussions are best approached**. "Should we address them in bed," she asked, "because that's where sex takes place?" Most marriage authors suggest someplace *other than in bed*. Some couples who have chairs or a couch near the bed can talk well there, but alone in the living room or at the kitchen table works better. A place away from the bed helps keep these discussions warm and loving.

Confession: In years past, my feelings about our sex life often spilled out just before we were *supposed* to make love. Picture a weepy girl in her birthday suit, conflicted about this particular episode. "I'm sorry, Honey, but I really want to talk something out first." Now picture a confused, misled, disappointed husband! You guessed it, the encounter usually didn't happen. I didn't *mean* to sabotage us. I wanted our time to be better, not worse. But, boy, was my timing off! Part of the problem, besides being a card-carrying coward, was that I didn't think about or plan a convenient time to talk. And sex rarely registered on my radar during meals.

I allowed the bed to change from a place of *wonderful* to a place of *conflict*. What about you? If the bedroom has been a place of spoken or unspoken tension, simply stop *ever discussing anything of any weight there*. Turn your bedroom into a place of affirmation and smiling joy. Touch, nuzzle, spoon. Tell your husband how much you appreciate his love. I'm so grateful I made the adjustment – but not nearly as glad as he is.

Samantha learned to tell her husband her sexual preferences *and*, just as importantly, her turn-offs. She even asked him to read this chapter with her ("Uh, sure," he said with a grin). Reading this subchapter with *your* hubby might start helpful conversations, and your courage in doing so might lead to some, shall we say, pleasant rewards.

We will discuss eight topics which cross gender lines. Men and women must communicate along these lines because neither husbands nor wives generally fall into any common preference.

Does the Setting Matter?

Usually one partner wants sex to sometimes be in a different place. Because memories of past exciting times fade, it's important to create new memories which bring a delicious sense of anticipation to the lovemaking session even if the setting is ho hum. Consider adding inexpensive splashes of color to the bedroom or bringing a lamp from another room. Be creative. Twinkle lights are cheap and easy to string on the headboard or an artificial tree. Fix up the guest room for a special chocolate dessert. Have you ever set up a picnic in the living room? If you save your extra change or single dollar bills, you can kidnap him for a night in a local hotel, including room service, of course, and a late checkout!

While we're talking about changing the setting for lovemaking, assure him of his skill as a lover. He will probably be more excited about a new location.

1. How do you feel about making love in a different place – sometimes? What ideas will you try first? _____

_____

_____

_____

_____

Who's More Spontaneous?

Are men generally more spontaneous than women? Possibly. We wives tend to prefer the anticipation and planning for lovemaking; but isn't there something sexy about *planned spontaneity*? For instance, quickies, which normally mean fast sex for his benefit, can be thought of differently. Bring a fresh air of excitement and passion by surprising the other for a quickie. We learned of a certain husband who pulled into the driveway one night and cut the engine. When his wife started passionately kissing him, they didn't get into the house for a few more minutes. A spontaneous moment became a great memory.

Now we've already discussed the Dimestore Quickie, the one for hubby's benefit. If the practice becomes routine, sex will surely die. But let me ask you, doesn't the thought of surprising your husband with a spontaneous, fifteen-minute rendezvous sound interesting? Try being spontaneous, for him, on purpose.

Scheduled, relaxed sex lends itself to a longer time of enjoyment and shouts the truth: *Sex is important enough to plan!* However, beware of letting a routine day or time for sex lull you into boredom. If you stop mentally preparing throughout the day for the time you've set, sex will soon fall by the wayside. Change your schedule every month or two, and make a holiday, vacation, or date night special by thinking and planning ahead.

2. *Who* is the more spontaneous mate? How will you make adjustments for either planning or allowing for more spontaneity? _____

_____

_____

_____

Is Privacy a Big Deal?

Impulsive describes men, especially when they're young. They might even forget to check if the door is *closed*, much less locked. But as years pass, husbands value privacy as much as women, and sometimes more so. The sensitivity to privacy issues often goes unexpressed until one partner makes the other hopping mad. We need to talk about this.

One partner may be jolted at the thought of being *seen*, while the other might be obsessed with the possibility of being *heard*. Getting privacy issues right is so psychologically important that some women (or men) refuse to have sex because of such fears. Over time, our thoughts and feelings change on the topic, so revisit the conversation as needed.

One huge issue is teenagers in the home. The very thought of their presence within fifty yards can throw a wrench into the master bedroom delights. This problem can keep some couples from engaging at all. Whoa! The marriage suffers if you drop sex because of privacy concerns. Be creative if you have teens. Try a once-a-month overnight away for the kids or weekend getaway for the two of you. Either one would breathe new vitality into your love life. Use teen nights at church or their social events to grab special time together.

3. *H*ow do you feel about privacy? How have you handled the issue? ____

_____

_____

_____

Does Variety Make a Difference?

The empty nest provides a new freedom. Which of you enjoys variety during foreplay or the act of lovemaking? What better time than now to get adventurous? Ask him where he'd like to start. A new position? A new order of procedure?

For their thirtieth anniversary at the beach, Sally and her husband found a romantic station in the car radio and got out onto the sand for a time of slow dancing. How long do you think that little tidbit of foreplay worked its magic in this couple's life? A long time.

Do you wonder what fifties-something woman would harbor such a silly romantic notion? Hopefully, it would be you. Another couple makes a point of doing something sexually different every anniversary. Be adventurous and mark one day each month when you will plan something different. The smallest change in routine counts. It takes thought – but you both will appreciate the added spark of remembering it later.

My husband and I added variety to our routine in a way which didn't require any creative thinking at the time. We planned ahead with the "**Idea Jar.**" We each wrote on colored notecards about six or seven foreplay plans we thought would be fun and put them in a mason jar. He said it shocked him that such a hokey idea could get his juices flowing… but it did.

If you try this and he writes an idea you don't feel comfortable with, kindly and gently ask him why that activity appeals to him. The conversation may create tension, so offer to think about it for a week, then choose another card. The tension should dissipate quickly with a new form of fun on the menu.

4. *R*ate yourself from 1 to 10 on your desire or willingness to try new things. Talk about how you might bring up this conversation. (In the next chapter we'll add plenty to this discussion.)_____

_____

_____

_____

_____

What's Your Optimum Time of Day?

The perfect time for love-making can be a big deal. Are you a nighttime lover? Possibly your husband likes morning best. Studies show that testosterone peaks in a man's body between 5:00 a.m. and 7:00 a.m. That's when he has a clear mind and desire for you — and you are quite likely sound asleep! Oh, dear… but it's a great opportunity to work on selflessness, sacrifice, and adapting.

Those words aren't written lightly. I winced while writing them. Waking from a sound sleep to respond to your mate's touch can seem not only unreasonable, but practically impossible. You might relate to Kate who instituted the rule: no morning sex. Whether or not sex happened later, how might such a rule impact the spirit of the relationship? Might a man feel that such a rule *ruled out* something special?

5. *W*hat do you think?_____

_____

_____

_____

This is not a unique problem. Another class member, Maddy, struggled for years with her husband's love of morning sex — not quickie sex, he wanted to enjoy real love-making with her. As the higher-drive mate, she almost never refused his advances, but she grew a big, cumbersome crop of resentment. His preference made her feel rushed and barely turned on. With young human voices already clanging and banging in the kitchen, she knew that in a few minutes the day would officially begin. Missing *their moment* sometimes brought tears.

When we asked Maddy how she handled her situation, she said, "This problem has forced me to cling to the Lord more than any other issue in our marriage. Before I pray, I have to get my attitude right about my husband, believing he cares deeply for me. I really want to scream, so it takes time to calm down. I've also tried to set an alarm and get up earlier to move around and be fully awake for him. But when I do that I end up failing, because that's the morning *he* decides to sleep. I have no answer. Maybe one day his morning hormones will ease up." As she talked about taking this matter to the Lord, we all felt convicted.

In another scenario, if you fall asleep at 10:00 p.m. and he's ready for you at 11:00, you're in a large club. Have you talked about it? We do ourselves a favor to negotiate first, then adopt the motto, "Adapt as much as possible." If you need help with this, I suggest asking a close friend to hold you accountable. Answer the question: Did I talk to or adapt to my man this week? Or did I bow out of sex because his timing didn't match mine?

6. *How* does *optimum time* play into your love life? Write the time preferences of both of you below. How have you handled these irritations in the past? What will you do differently now? _____

_____

_____

_____

_____

Do You Want Sex More Often or More Time for Sex?

How does the higher-drive wife approach a husband whose tank registers full and hers sits on empty? He likes sex – possibly a lot. Just not as often. Maybe sex on the weekend is fine for him, both physically and emotionally. If you, however, need a check-in during the week, you probably feel lonely, frustrated, and rejected.

Though already mentioned, the problem warrants a bit more discussion here. Because of men's stereotypical higher sex drive, society hints at a double standard which makes women naturally good, and men naturally bad where sex is concerned. If a man once used women for sexual physical release, he may not understand the mutuality of marital sex, or that sex as God designed it is totally good. Some men report feeling *happy* the wife is available for sex, but can't help comparing her to highly-sexualized women in pornography. Surely his *good wife* doesn't *need* sex or act too eager. This attitude may be yet another of the tragic results of pornography.

Again, shame enters the picture. A man must be freed from shame in order to properly value his wife's appropriate sexual enthusiasm. When men see their wives as both wholesome and sexual beings with a strong desire for joy-filled lovemaking, they are *normal* men. A counselor may help talk through the issue.

Sex fulfills many emotional needs for wives. You may want to be comforted through sex. You may need a time of relaxation fully away from pressures and duties. You may have deep needs for reassurance of his affection. You ask, "Do you value me enough – am I attractive enough – will you meet my need even when *you* don't need sex?"

It takes courage and determination to open the conversation or make the moves. Fear of rejection sits on your chest like a brick. He has no idea how his passivity or rejection hurts you. Try asking, "How about it, Honey? You know I will have a quickie even at 5:00 a.m. But will you also take time for relaxed lovemaking during the week – preferably in the evening? I really need more time to feel fulfilled. How about an extra half hour next time?"

Here's the tough part. Walk away from the conversation without expecting an immediate response. Pray, trusting the Lord to give you confidence in who you are as a woman, a wife, a lover. The attitude *will* come through to him. Ask an accountability friend to help you pray about keeping your heart soft as you work through this difference of timing and need.

7. If you are the higher-drive wife, how will you seek help from both the Lord and a friend? How will you make sure you don't suffer alone? _____

_____

_____

_____

_____

What About Grooming Issues?

How blessed the woman whose husband values his physical desirability for lovemaking! Women like *Squeaky Clean,* so before *special time,* it's always appropriate to check out how each other feels about a shower first.

When either mate is tempted to refuse the other a moment of spontaneity because they don't feel fresh and clean, an appropriate response would be, "Hey, let me take a quick jump into the shower." Rescheduling for a later time may work too, but be sensitive. Don't abuse your freedom in this area.

What a good place to address the topic of hair, right? We all know men's hair increases all over their body as they get older, while women's grows thinner. Traditionally, men get hair groomed at the barbershop or salon, ie. neck, face, head. When I read this section to my guy, he added a mandate to pass on the following advice: Men must deal with *some hair issues* at home! Ear hair, bushy eyebrows, even torso hair can turn a woman off, big time. My man considers his razor, trimmer, scissors, and nail clippers very close friends. At the risk of TMI (too much info), I will say he shaves and trims *lots* of places on his body – for the enhancement of his aging physique. And I do appreciate it.

8. *H*ave you talked about these issues with your man? Has cleanliness interfered with your love life? At this point, how do feel about inviting your husband into the shower with you? _____

_____

_____

_____

What About Love Languages?

Dr. Gary Chapman, author of *The Five Love Languages,*[6] mentored Walt and me in our early marriage. His book popularized the concept of learning how our loved ones want to be loved. Since we know our own love language, we have a tendency to love our children and mate the way *we* want to be loved. A problem develops when the other person doesn't feel loved. We're not loving him in his language.

Right from the start of the love affair, this difference shows up. Even after decades of marriage, our love language can change and cause rifts. When a thoughtful gift once brought a thrill, it's now quality time that makes his or her heart sing. Where words of encouragement once created the perfect evening, now he prefers acts of service (like help with a home project).

The languages of love are gender-neutral. Ask him, "Hey babe, what's your current love language?" Rate each one, from most to least important, giving the highest value a 1.

Your Preferred Love Language	Your Husband's
a._____ Physical Touch and Closeness	_____
b._____ Encouraging Words	_____
c._____ Quality Time	_____
d. _____ Gifts	_____
e._____ Acts of Service	_____

9. *H*ow have your love languages changed over the years? _____

_____

_____

_____

_____

10. *H*ave you thought of other differences and preferences regarding your sex life? _____

_____

_____

11. *W*hat about the amount of time taken for any lovemaking session? __

_____

_____

_____

12. *W*hat about pillow talk just before or during sex? Would you rather your lover talked more during a rendezvous, or less? _____

_____

_____

13. *D*o you, should you, use bedroom time to bring up the kids? _____

_____

_____

*S*hare your thoughts about any preference issue not mentioned here. Marriage means navigating change at the core of your love life. Embrace and negotiate change. It's the only constant in our world. _____

_____

_____

_____

_____

_____

_____

Ten Occasions Making Love is a Good Idea

*R*emember when you were first married? You needed no occasion to make love. You made time for sex as a matter of normal life. In fact, the mere idea of being reminded to engage made no sense. Funny how years change us.

Whether you agree with all or only a few of these suggestions for lovemaking, look at them as a friendly reminder. More lovemaking gives us a greater sense of youthfulness and may even delay some aspects of aging. So go ahead, grab some bonus years. Write your responses to these ideas and discuss them in your group so you can form goals for the future. For fun, circle the suggestions you've never thought of in the past, but will consider now.

Before Overnight Guests Arrive and After They Leave

First, you need extra energy to entertain company. Though sex takes some energy, it's physiologically proven to boost energy — like a mild workout at the gym. Do you exercise for more energy? Sex also gives that boost plus the closeness you need for the arrival of guests. Soon you'll both be busy serving in different ways and going different directions.

If you've made love recently, you'll be a better team when the house fills up. For example, while the company chats away, Hubby may catch your eye across the room. Maybe he'll wink and smile that smile that says, "You're the best." After the taillights disappear from the driveway and the house is all yours again, collapse into a cuddle. You deserve it.

1. *H*ow does having company affect your love life?_____

_____

_____

_____

After You've Had a Fight

Nothing says we're friends again like the benediction of lovemaking. Remember how sex used to clear the air after a fight and bring you back into the same boat again? With kisses, you reassured each other all is well despite your differences of opinion and misunderstandings.

Why, after several decades, do we tend to skip this part of conflict? What happens when we no longer have *makeup sex*? Instead of fighting out an issue, we often just stuff it away in the I-don't-care part of our heart.

Fighting may not top your fun list, but fighting used to be worth the making up. Lovemaking was the immediate reward for getting to the heart of the matter – I love you, even though we disagree. These days, it might take a conversation and a decision for one of you to initiate makeup sex after a conflict. If he doesn't do it, you do it.

2. *O*n a scale of 1 to 10, rate your ability to end a conflict well. How will you address the issue of ending a fight? _____

_____

_____

_____

After a Trip, Sickness, or Injury

When we'd been married just a few years, a brush fire sent my husband to the hospital with severe burns. After his discharge a week later, his hands and neck bandaged… yes, even with bandages, he wanted a proper welcome home! Though a bit caught off guard that day, I came to realize that *back to normal* means lovemaking. Absence or abstinence makes the heart grow fonder, right?

Sure, hormones wane. Sure, you may not *need* sex, but why not welcome each other home in the same way, in *this* season? You might not realize it, but when the two of you fall back to regular busy life after an illness or returning home, one of you probably feels out of sorts or off rhythm. Patient or caregiver, traveler or the one left behind, we do well to pause, put ourselves in the other's shoes, and give a warm welcome back.

3. *W*hen did you last make love to say "welcome home"?_____

_____

_____

_____

When Your Kids Drop Some News

…like expecting their third child in four years or joining the Army. Grown kids can throw curve balls. You weren't prepared for that marriage announcement or the decision to move out of the country. Yes, you know this is their life, and it will be difficult, as yours has been. We have to pull ourselves up short and resist the urge to get emotionally tangled up in all the unknowns waiting around the bend. We have to remind ourselves all the time to stop obsessing about the grown kids!

It's your time now – a time with less drama and more predictability. Get to the sweet drama in your bedroom and celebrate your separate-from-the-kids life. When it comes right down to it, what your grown kids need from you more than anything else (except prayer) is your model of a great love life. Your love for each other means more to them than your advice. Way more.

181

4. When were you tempted to let the grown kids throw your lovemaking off course? How did you recover? _____

_____

_____

_____

When Discouraged or Overwhelmed

Sex can comfort like nothing else (except maybe chocolate). When difficulties happen at work, at church, or with aging parents, each of you needs to know your partner will tenderly lift up your chin, take your hand, and point you toward the couch. Oxytocin helps a sad heart. Take time to snuggle. Afterward, a long back rub and tender kisses can usher in a time of deep healing. Don't underestimate the *balm* you have in your fingertips for a hurt psyche. Some couples look back on a time like this and hardly remember the pain; they remember the cure.

5. Tell of a time you encouraged your husband (or he encouraged you) through tender touch. _____

_____

_____

_____

When a Movie or Sunset Brings You Close

It's too easy to let movies fill our need for romance vicariously. *Technology Pseudo-life*, my term for vicarious living in a world of affluence, drives our society more than any in the past. How sad that so many have no other romantic life than the one they see in the media.

Wholesome on-screen romance, however, can work for us in our real lives. If we think of what we can have if we work hard on our relationship, a good romantic movie can propel us into each other's arms. But this doesn't happen naturally. That kind of response must be cultivated by choosing to *act* on romantic thoughts and feelings brought on by happy happenings. We must choose to celebrate the closeness we feel after a promotion or a big sale or a new car.

Move away from vicarious living over into the fulfilling world of your own making – a real one.

6. *How* will you start to rethink the romantic feelings which come from a beautiful sunset or movie? _____

_____

_____

_____

_____

On Saturday Mornings

So you haven't made love all week? What a great time! In the past, your sweet encounter had to compete with cartoons in the living room or clanging cereal bowls in the kitchen. Not now.

Sure, the lawn must be mowed, leaves raked, house cleaned. Taking care of your marriage, though, should go to the top of the Home Maintenance List. When you get to the poem, *Just One Hour More*, at the end of the book, be inspired to grab a leisurely morning once a month. Maintain your love life first and see how all the rest gets done with more gusto. If one Saturday you stay in bed until dinner, no problem. It will all still be there for you next week.

7. *When* have you enjoyed just such a Saturday? If you haven't, when will you put one on the calendar? _____

_____

_____

_____

Vacations or Holidays

You'd think this would be the most natural time for a couple to emotionally connect; but many take a vacay from their love life while on vacation. Have you tucked away a mental album of holiday love? Start one this year. Begin to put part of a vacation day (or staycation) off limits for a relaxed morning or afternoon respite. Take a walk alone. You have people to see, plans for meals, picnics, outings. Just add a little pocket of time for each other. The holiday may turn out less stressful.

I remember when we used to have our Thanksgiving meal at 1:00. We'd both get up at five to stuff the turkey. We'd put it into the oven, and I'd do a little victory dance back to the bedroom. Household still asleep, cool air outside our covers, both of us wide awake. Boy, oh, boy!

The way our minds work, a sexual encounter on a holiday will be remembered just because it happened *on that day*. And those kinds of memories keep us younger, happier, and motivated to make sex a priority.

8. *What* upcoming holiday will you choose to find time for a short break from the festivities? How will you do it? _____

_____

_____

_____

A Rainy Day

Texas doesn't get much rain. When we wake up to dark clouds and the unfamiliar rumbling of thunder, it really sets a crawl-back-into-bed mood. If the day happens to fall on a weekend, I often say, "Well, a lot of babies will be made today!"

If you think of lovemaking as the sunshine of the marriage, you get a picture of how the relationship can begin to wilt without both sun and rain. The garden inside our hearts needs the water of oxytocin regularly. So, on a rainy day, grab the chance to shut out the world. Close the curtains, listen to the patter on the roof, put on some romantic music, brew a cup of hot tea, and head back to bed.

9. *S*hare a memory of a rainy day of love. How will you revisit the idea again soon? _____

_____

_____

_____

When It's Been Awhile

How long is *your awhile*? For some it's a few days, for others a few weeks. How long has it been?

- If you can't remember, it's been too long.
- If you identify the time and place using a month and year, it's been too long. "Well, let's see. I seem to remember that vacation in June, 2011..."
- If you just can't be bothered, it's been too long.
- If you are fuming about something that happened over a month ago, it's been too long.
- If you feel rejected and ignored, it's been too long. Make the first move.
- If you can hardly remember the sense of well-being lovemaking produces, it has been too long.

10. *H*ow long is your *too long*? Share here how you hope to change it. _____

_____

_____

_____

_____

10

A Time to Practice, Practice, Practice

Four Women and "The 'O' Grid"

1 Peter 5:7

 *"...Casting all your care upon Him, for He cares for you..."*

Blake, Mindy, Emma, and Betsy were college friends twenty-three years ago. The story of their reunion and candid sharing will help illustrate the four quadrants of the grid below. But before we hear from them, in the grid below, what does "emotionally involved" mean to you? Enthusiasm for today's lovemaking? Or a warm, ongoing feeling of being in love? For our purposes, emotional involvement may mean either one or both, depending on different circumstances in our seasons of marriage. Also, just in case you didn't know what the "O" meant before you saw the grid, it's a common euphemism for orgasm — the big "O."

	No Climax	Climax
Emotionally Involved		
Not Emotionally Involved		

This chapter will challenge you to understand how important practice is to your love life! As a matter of fact, two main factors make practice of any worthwhile activity enjoyable: *regularity and emotional involvement.* Think of any sport or job – or even church attendance. If we engage regularly and work toward enjoyment, practice may turn to delight. We hope the stories of these four women challenge you to make practice in your love life a priority.

Emma was the *spark plug* who found the other three gals on social media, rekindled their friendship through a year of sporadic pictures and posts, and launched a plan to get them together. They agreed to meet for a girls' weekend in Albuquerque, Emma's home, for what she called "a surprise."

When she picked the three up at the airport, Emma kept the suspense going. Their animated conversation made the three-hour drive to the surprise seem like a short hop. When they landed at a beautiful resort tucked in the middle of nowhere, Emma revealed her surprise. They'd be attending a women's retreat with the theme *Close Encounters of the Marital Kind.*

What?! You're kidding! Oh, well. Too late to turn back now.

They carried their suitcases down a winding path to a series of tiny log cabins equipped with a fireplace and two sets of bunks each. The brightly-colored Southwest decor raised the atmosphere well above teencamp level. After settling in, the women found the vaulted, beamed-ceiling lodge where leather couches surrounded an enormous rock fireplace. *Wow. Nice.*

The opening session with sixty or so attendees ended as the ladies received paper and envelopes. They were instructed to write their most troubling issues regarding sexual intimacy and seal them until the final night.

Their "confessional" didn't turn out to be difficult at all, for over the weekend the women had deepened their bond of trust, even more so than in college days. Here are their Envelope Issues, followed by my comments.**

Top Left Quadrant: Emotionally Involved, No Orgasm.

Betsy: *"I'll go first, but this is so hard. I have a good husband! He is patient and kind, as well as a good dad. When we met, two years post-graduate, we got married quickly and I had no idea what to expect with sex – and we got pregnant right away. During those months, I felt awkward, worried if sex was okay for the baby and if I should even be having fun. Then the next year, yikes, I got pregnant again. Fast forward two more babies, add a crazy busy life, and orgasm just didn't happen.*

"I wrote on my paper that Dan wants to know how he can make sex better, but I don't even know what an orgasm is supposed to be like! Am I messed up down there? I feel like a failure! We do the same thing over and over, and it's not working. Now, Dan is starting to give up. One of us will initiate sex maybe once a month because we get some feeling of connection from it. But the pain of my blocked libido is getting to us both. Help!

1. Why do you think Hollywood movies portray sexual fulfillment as an automatic response for women who love their husbands?_____

_____

_____

**No matter how attracted to or emotionally engaged with our mate, orgasm for women sometimes take education, patience, and a lot of kissing and touching. In this chapter we will give you more tips, but here's the most important one: whether you have ever had an orgasm or not, simply make pleasure your goal. Your body is like no other, yet common to all in the respect that it can experience sensual delight ordained by God.

After learning about her body, Betsy needs to communicate to her hubby what she'd like to try. All men must be assured that her orgasm during intercourse doesn't prove his masculinity nor does it necessarily trump orgasm produced by a tender touch in the right places. When this burden rolls off his back, the two can work toward orgasm in other creative ways.

Once learned, orgasm may elude during certain periods of a marriage: during the vaginal dryness of perimenopause, with teens in a room nearby, or no known reason whatsoever. If we stay present, engaged in the moment, even when orgasm seems out of reach, the good times will come back. We can't say it enough: each moment of pleasure, even without orgasm, feeds your imagination for the next encounter. Imagine how you'd love to touch your mate, how you'd love him to touch you. This brings us to the next quadrant.

Lower Right Quadrant: No Emotional Involvement, but with Orgasm.

Emma: *"Well, I guess I'll go next. I have always had easy orgasms. I masturbated as a teen as well as had both serious and casual sexual relationships, so I knew what to expect when I married Stan. But, sadly, we haven't had a good relationship. I wrote on my paper that I would like to fall in love with him rather than wish he would change. Not that he's a bad husband. I'm just not attracted to him anymore. Maybe it's because fishing excites him way more than being with me.*

We can go as long as six weeks without sex, but I can always climax because of two things: one, he knows exactly how to touch me, and two, I always fantasize some scene elsewhere. After we finish, he thinks we are fine. He has no idea that in the past ten or so years, fantasizing has become my only way of climaxing.

"So what do I do? He doesn't talk to me intimately or enjoy our new grandbaby; he golfs almost every weekend or goes fishing for days at a time in the wilderness. But I know none of that is really the problem. I am the problem. My heart is cold."

**Orgasm for Emma is just a skill.

2. *W*hat factors do you think contributed to Emma's lack of emotional involvement? _____

_____

_____

3. *S*hould she talk through her situation with Stan? If not, why, and to whom do you think she should talk? _____

_____

_____

When you think or dream about yourself and your husband in a romantic setting, you are enhancing the pleasure of your moment together. If Emma could soften her heart toward Stan, she might be able to indulge in the profitable kind of fantasizing – and stop imagining sex with other people in other places. We call the escaping kind of fantasy **dissociation**. Though controversy on the topic exists among therapists, most Christian counselors agree the erotic boost of dissociating doesn't build a lasting intimacy.

Think about how God made us. Deep in our hearts, all women (all people) crave relationship. We know orgasm doesn't replace a heart connection, but it can function apart from one. Might your skill in achieving orgasm have nothing to do with intimacy? Do you avoid the emotional component of lovemaking, go elsewhere mentally, in order to protect your heart from hurt? Most women who do this eventually lose interest in sex altogether, because without emotion, sex morphs into an empty exercise.

Lower Left Quadrant: No Emotional Involvement, No Orgasm.

Blake: *"My turn? Might as well just say it, I used to have orgasms once in awhile, but now I fake them. I wasn't really into sex and got tired of the time it took to get there, so I began this shortcut quite a few years ago. It used to be mostly laziness, but now my husband's sex drive drives me crazy! Don't get me wrong… he's a good guy, a good dad, a good provider – he just needs more sex than I can ever keep up with. I have no time to build any interest on my own. None, zip. Any interest left long ago, and Tom doesn't seem to care whether my response is real or not. We have a routine where I can tell he's close to his climax. Then my fake one signals his turn to… So in effect, sex is over when I decide and he doesn't have to feel guilty. Lately, it's over pretty quick.*

"Ugh… you guys must think I'm horrible. After this weekend, though, I think maybe I should tell him and let the chips fall where they may. I wrote on my paper that I want to stop faking, but I didn't write down the telling him part. If I tell him, what will happen to my marriage?"

**Blake opted for the simple, though dishonest and unsatisfying solution to a sexual dilemma. Many women's occasional deceit has nothing to do with a husband's frequency of wanting sex. Faking is merely the easy route to finish and move on to the next thing.

4. *I*s there such a thing as sexual laziness? Have you ever faked the occasional orgasm or have you gotten into the habit? How did it start? What results have you seen?_____

_____

_____

_____

5. *D*o you think Blake should tell her husband about her habit? Why or why not?

_____

_____

_____

If you relate to Blake, you may decide to stop the practice of faking without mentioning it to your husband. But if he were faking, would you want to know? Also, would you be concerned or curious if he suddenly changed how he related to you during sex? While men's egos are generally super-sensitive in this area, your husband may surprise you with his support after learning the struggle you've had. Connie, our reluctant hopeful from Chapter 1, knew a heart connection ideally precedes an orgasmic response, so she opened up to her husband and discussed all her fears and issues with him.

Many factors contribute to a wife's lack of emotional involvement. She may be overloaded with outside stress or conflict; other priorities may crowd out pleasure right now. Fears related to her sexuality or the husband's might seem debilitating. Possibly, her husband may hurry her through sex (Chapter 2, Sexually Stuck Women – When Sex is All About Him). After recovering from a prolonged illness, a couple might not feel connected. At such times we can't give up. We must believe better days lie ahead; we must pray, talk, then pray some more.

But if you have yet to experience orgasm, know that faking won't get you to the other side. Besides possibly killing the spirit of the marriage, it will set you back farther in your quest for emotional and sexual fulfillment.

Remember one main premise of our study: Taking the time to learn how to enjoy your husband's sexual touch can serve as a door to emotional closeness.

A Time to Practice, Practice, Practice

For more helps besides the great books on our AWE Book List, the website **To Love, Honor, And Vacuum by Sheila Wray Gregoire** has thoroughly organized and categorized articles on the sexual relationship.[1]

It's important to note here that seeking professional counsel is never a sign of failure. On the contrary, not seeking help can sometimes most surely mean failure. Your marriage is meant to impact the world for good – so get the help you need. Which brings us to the last quadrant.

Upper Right Quadrant: Emotional Involvement with Orgasm

Mindy: *"Pete is several years older than me, but man, he is an awesome lover! We have a crazy good sex life. We laugh together a lot, and I'm so glad we can talk about everything that concerns us – especially our love life. He never expects me to climax every time we make love, and it's easy for me to say, "Hey, Babe, I'm fine not having one today."*

It's not that he's the most romantic guy in the world; it's just that he prioritizes our sex life. He even installed two shower heads in our bathroom remodel so we could stay in the shower together longer! (I like the water a lot hotter than he does.)

But there's a slight catch. I wrote on my paper that I worry. I love sex with this man, but his back trouble and other physical issues keep interrupting our groove, if ya know what I mean. Sometimes I wonder if this will be the year our party ends. I guess I'm selfish. Sex refreshes our souls. But, between his pain and doctor visits, I stay uptight. I know it's wrong to harbor this fretting! I just want our love life to last longer!

**This final quadrant where Mindy and Pete live is, of course, the place we want to live too. Can you relate to their passion? Yet how sad when our enemy pulls out the fear trick when his other tricks fail to drive us apart. Joy can't quite find a home in our hearts if in the back of our minds a constant, nagging worry hounds us – the fear *our party* will soon end. It takes a determined effort to *cast all our cares on him.* Do we really believe God cares?

Women usually pass through and camp a while in all four quadrants of The "O" Grid. We either withhold emotional involvement while having a lot of subpar sex, or we stop having regular sex because it seems to have failed us.

Thankfully, God places deep within us a desire for a closer bond with our man and a warm sexual response. When times of emotional detachment come, will you look reality straight in the face and choose to reconnect? Take one day at a time, *"casting all your cares on him, for he cares for you.* (1 Peter 5:7)

6. *What* do you see as you look back at your love life from the vantage point of these four quadrants? _____

_____

_____

_____

We still have more to learn as we continue on our journey. Pray today for a renewed commitment to be more emotionally involved in each sexual encounter. God designed your relationship to be good even as it experiences ups and downs. Thank him for opening your heart to all he has for you. ___

_____

_____

_____

_____

_____

_____

Tips for the First Ten Minutes of Sex

Song of Solomon 2:14b
"...show me your face, let me hear your voice;
your voice is sweet, and your face is lovely."

Fran and her husband plan lovemaking twice a week on specific days. Why? Because planned sex, though not better than spontaneous sex, sure beats no sex. Their busy work schedules and two six-foot boys in the house make scheduling a necessity. Spontaneous sex is always an option, but they want to relax and enjoy each other with all pistons firing. If they inadvertently miss the first day of the schedule, they have the second one to fall back on.

Their mid-week appointment falls on Fran's day off. Her morning includes doctor appointments, shopping, and haircuts. After lunch, she takes an hour nap, thinking about what she'd like to do later. She anticipates. As you might expect, by the time these two lovers eat dinner and *retire* for the evening, Fran has her mind in the right place. The two then take an hour to just talk before *serious* foreplay begins. This bonding time produces the oxytocin which makes sex better.

196

Do you sometimes fall behind in sexual arousal and yet hesitate to speak up to your hubby? Without coming across critical of his lovemaking, we'd love a bit more nuzzling, kissing, and hugging before the main event. Maybe he would, too. Though his physical system may work at lightning speed, his emotional system mirrors yours. He needs to feel your connection. He will appreciate everything, and I mean everything, you do to make sex better for yourself.

Here are a few ideas for slowing things down a bit. By adding ten minutes to pre-foreplay, the oxytocin buildup will increase enjoyment for both of you.

Get Undressed Slower

Of course this *could* be counterproductive and actually speed things up! The idea is to do something different in the process of undressing. Maybe ask for help with a certain article of clothing. You just added **at least another minute...**

Touch Up the Room

Yes, do this without your clothes. Whether your hour to engage may be Sunday afternoon, mid-evening, or early morning, darken the room a little, or maybe suggest the guest room. The idea of a different place may be all your engine needs to rev. Light a candle or two to make you look better to each other. Put on some soft music. You've now added about **four more minutes** to your repertoire.

Get a Tiny Snack or Drink for the Bedroom

"Oh, I forgot! I have a treat for us. Just give me a quick minute..." Slip into a robe (or not) and go to the kitchen to pour some pink lemonade or wine in small glasses. If your guy falls asleep during this interlude, it may work to your advantage when he awakens bleary-eyed to the vision of wine and a naked woman. **Voila, three more minutes!**

Use the Bathroom

Do this regularly just before sex, because it may help prevent a UTI from intercourse. As our bladder ages, we're much more sensitive to the urge to go. So go again with little or no clothing. While out of the room, offer up a grateful heart, anticipate, and ponder what would feel great. We've just added **another two minutes**, but let's try to get three more…

Talk a Little While You Kiss

While sipping your drinks, squeeze his muscles and compliment his body. Some men might want to speed up the process, but most fellows will slow down to hear certain words. Talk about something he did today you found helpful or admirable. Tell him he's a great lover. These words will not only mean much to him, they will accomplish even more for *you*. They get your head more into the moment. **Whether you talk or don't talk, you already added ten minutes. Good for you!**

*S*hare here your routine before making love. How will you change it to extend the anticipation? _____

_____

_____

_____

_____

_____

Nine Tips for Better Practice

I Corinthians 13:4, 5

"Love is patient and kind... it does not insist on its own way."

Tip 1: Change Your Definition of Sex

After reading the previous chapters, has your definition of sex changed? You will probably not feel free to delve into the tips ahead unless you are willing to expand your thoughts and beliefs about biblical sexuality. It takes a decision. Am I willing to work on my marriage in this area? According to Romans 12:1 and 2,[1] we are to sacrifice our bodies and renew our minds. Have you ever read those verses in a marital or sexual light? If sex is about serving my husband in sacrificial love, as well as about my pleasure, how do these verses change your understanding of sex?

1. Write your new definition of sex.

_____

_____

_____

A Time to Practice, Practice, Practice

Tip 2: Read Good Books

Restoring the Pleasure by Clifford and Joyce Penner[2] is a great resource. The Penners, trusted Christian sex therapists, have written prolifically. Pick up any book by this couple for answers to your toughest sexual problems.

Also, Sheila Wray Gregoire's ebook, *31 Days to Great Sex*,[3] will set the stage for lovemaking in a practical, paced progression. Our AWE Book List, separated into sections, has a goldmine of help for your particular needs. Reading a Christian sex/marriage book a year will not only promote a more fulfilling lovelife, a couple will grow emotionally and spiritually closer as they continue to learn. Approach this idea gingerly by reading aloud a paragraph from a book you think he'd like. Then see what happens.

No matter how much we read and listen to podcasts, we'll never feel we've arrived.

2. *W*hich book will you start first? _____

_____

_____

_____

Tip 3: Plan "His" Nights and "Her" Nights

After dinner, hand him an invitation to **His Night**. The card might read something like this, "Honey, meet me in the bedroom at 9:00 in your birthday suit. I'll dress the same and let you know my plan for your **His Night** then." Would any guy turn down this invitation?

When you arrive, offer to be the giver of your husband's sexual wishes. Note: on His Night **you have no pressure to respond sexually**. That's part of the deal. You observe and give.

Some women begin to feel new sexual feelings during His Nights. The brain is funny that way. It can respond when pressure fades away. If you get aroused, see where it takes you as you seek to give him all the attention.

On another appointed evening, plan a **Her Night**. Once he knows what's going to happen, he won't need any extra time, but give him a couple of days to anticipate. Prepare the room in any way you think will enhance your romantic, sensual feelings. At the appointed time, lie on your back or stomach or side wearing anything you think will turn you on. **He is to be at your beck and call. Would you like him to brush your hair, give you a foot rub, or a shoulder massage? He may not expect you to do anything for him.** If he asks permission to do this or that, you have full right to decline and redirect him.

This is when you may have the elusive orgasm. Be sure to relax. If you want intercourse at some point on these evenings, by all means indulge; but don't lose sight of the point. This is YOUR turn to take pleasure and give instructions, with no hurry of arousal. So, go for it! Prepare a few hours ahead with pelvic floor exercises, a bubble bath, prayer, and time to daydream.

Finally, remember that to ask for a time of intimate touching is okay, even if, presently, **your husband isn't functioning well sexually**. Does the idea sound selfish to you? It isn't. When a wife courageously asks her husband for this favor, they are usually amazed at the feeling of renewed closeness they both feel afterward. **The husband also experiences a surprising rush of oxytocin!** If you need the words to ask, here's a start.

> Honey, we've gone a while without sex because of health issues right now, and you may not want to go there because you think things won't work right. I get it – but, Babe, we're going to get through this! I read how we can do something to help us both. It's supposed to give you a great feeling when you help me climax, and it would sure encourage me right now. Just think about it…

3. *How* do you feel about this practice tip? If you are hesitant to initiate a **His Night** night, think about where your feelings might have come from. When you are ready, write down a target date for this event and compose your invitation here. _____

_____

_____

_____

Tip 4: Learn in the Perpendicular Non-Demand Position

Unlike His Night or Her Night, the Perpendicular Non-Demand Position is more like therapy. In this exercise, the husband sits beside you (possibly cross-legged) while you lie on your back, knees slightly bent and raised by a rolled up blanket or pillow. Make sure the room is warm and comfortable. This position allows you to focus more completely on your sensations of pleasure.

Try this once a week if you are having trouble orgasming. It may take two or three hours to let go and orgasm. Sometimes the dedicated attention from a husband to the wife's pleasure is all it takes to carry her sexual experience over the top.

Intercourse isn't on the menu in this therapy. Using small amounts of genital-friendly massage oil, have him gently massage your torso using small strokes. He may or may not talk, but unlike Her Night, he must slow down even more than ever before, spending lots of time on legs, arms, and breasts, eventually working his way to labia and clitoris – when you are ready. Don't look at this like a spa massage. Tiny strokes all over make the difference.

At some point, though not necessarily the first time you try this exercise, arousal will take over, and you will orgasm. Clear your mind and allow enough time for good feelings. **The minute you feel bored, impatient, pain, or any other negative, take a break.** Perhaps get a drink and talk a few minutes.

4. Might this exercise help even the orgasmic wife? How? What reservations do you have with this therapy? _____

_____

_____

_____

Tip 5: Try Something Different

We've already talked about variety in the bedroom, but we need to talk about it again. Changing anything relating to sex is really tough. Since focused relaxation is the key to orgasm, wouldn't a change make both focus and relaxation more difficult? No, because the second most important ingredient in lovemaking is the "making" part – making a memory to fuel future moments.

Make changes in tiny increments. Suggest a bath or shower together, or enjoy an expensive chocolate truffle in bed. Simply switch bedrooms, go all the way on the couch, or hop into the car for a throwback to years gone by. The possibilities are endless. Check out ideas in *Red Hot Monogamy* by Bill and Pam Farrel. We really like #108.[4]

> "Revive Rome! Wrap yourself and your spouse in a toga (a bed sheet will make a nice one). Toss all kinds of pillows on the floor and then recline as you drop grapes into each other's mouths."

Also, consider trying new positions for intercourse. This alone may help you achieve orgasm. Pressure in just the right spot in just the right way is best found through experimentation. On an at-home date night try the **Idea Jar** we talked about earlier. Write out fun foreplay fantasies on colored cards and drop them into the jar. **Challenge: Draw one card out the first weekend of every month.**

5. *How* will you change something this week? _____

_____

_____

_____

Tip 6: Be Expressive, But Don't Spectate

Do I dare put an exclamation mark here? In their Christian sex manual, *The Married Guy's Guide to Great Sex*, Dr. Cliff and Joyce Penner[5] warn against either the husband or wife "spectatoring" during sex. When we wonder how we might look during a sexual encounter, we are spectatoring ourselves. We can also mess ourselves up by spectatoring our partner's sexual response.

This doesn't mean you leave lights off! Not at all. Nor does it mean you don't look into each other's eyes as you pleasure each other. It simply means you must not interrupt your good feelings to check each other out for how things are going. Your husband shouldn't wonder if he's making you happy. A flushed face from arousal isn't enough. Lubrication and engorgement of the labia aren't enough. You both need verbal involvement and expressive expressions and/or moans.

Most husbands love the sounds you make, so let it go. If you have thin walls, make sure to arrange for appropriate privacy. Be verbally encouraging. Tell him he's doing great when he is. If he's not, stop him. Keep the train moving forward, or take a break.

6. *W*hat do you think about adding the verbally expressive part of love-making? When you ask him if he'd like to hear more from you, report what he said here. _____

_____

_____

_____

Tip 7: Don't Get Hooked on Soft Porn or Batteries

Or novels, either. These "helps" claim to put couples into an erotic mood, but does the mood last? Do they provide an experience which builds the thrill of pure love? Relying on soft porn can trip the brain to become desensitized to normal relating. Couples eventually realize the mental images they replay during sex don't necessarily draw them closer emotionally. Though steamy passages in books may arouse us, they take us to a different time and place, away from today's real rendezvous.

Some husbands and wives also introduce battery-operated sex toys into the bedroom repertoire. Of course, no prohibition to these props can be found in the Bible. But be careful. Like pornography, any apparatus for achieving orgasm can create a dependence – and often does. Some women can't orgasm without the help of a vibrator or other device. When the two of you completely agree about extra items for your lovemaking, you have freedom. Just remember the whole point of sex is oneness, not sexual function.

Another common "help" for couples is self-pleasuring in the company of the other. What does a couple do who must be separated by long distances for long periods of time?

Might self-stimulation while thinking about the mate, help the couple manage such separation? The Bible says nothing about touching one's self. When helping build oneness between a married couple, Christian sex therapists may recommend this practice to hurdle a thorny issue in arousal.

The many exercises and therapies employed by the Penners in their sex manual *Restoring the Pleasure*[6] may help you avoid the need of a licensed sex therapist. God tells us in Hebrews 13:4 that marriage should "be held in honor among all, and let the marriage bed be undefiled…"

In determining what activities are off-limits by God's standards, four guidelines come from Christian marriage writers. We can ask the following questions.

- Is the activity prohibited in Scripture?
- Does the activity involve only the couple and no one else?
- Do both husband and wife want to participate?
- Does the activity restore or build up the oneness of the marriage?

If you can answer no, yes, yes, yes, to the above questions, go for it.

7. How has your past or recent experimentation with novels or toys affected your marriage?_____

_____

_____

_____

Tip 8: Touch Each Other Sexually
Five to Seven Minutes a Day

What?! Some men would not be able or willing to be sexual without having sex. The very thought seems crazy to them. But what do couples do when sex turns blah? Most will slowly stop having sex while worrying about their relationship – until the worry passes. And believe me, it does pass. After a certain age, no more sex becomes the route of least resistance, the easier way to live.

205

But what if couples committed to simply caress each other every day during dry, stale times? To touch in a way no one else can touch may be the only way of keeping the door open to each other's hearts.

Worrying about your sex life, on the other hand, spins a vicious cycle. We *can* accept *not climaxing* for awhile, but we shouldn't accept no sexual touch. Most older couples who don't give up on sex attest to the fact that blah times pass. Those who touch each other and focus on warm feelings restore desire.

Establish a habit of being sexual together a little bit every day. Warm kisses, gentle nuzzles, light massages – you get the idea. Without setting a timer, though that wouldn't be a bad idea at first, touch each other sensually for five to seven minutes every day.

When your husband struggles through a time of stress, touch him lovingly whether he reciprocates or not. Who knows? Maybe one day as you wake up in the morning or before you fall asleep, your caresses will usher in a flood of intoxicating oxytocin. Now, a powerful "want to" in one or both of you enters the picture. When that happens, you'll be ready to enjoy the full sexual experience again.

8. *Happy* couples develop a habit of being sexual. How will you start this new habit?_____

_____

_____

_____

Tip 9: Pray About Your Sex Life Every Day

My husband began to pray regularly for our sex life when our final child flew the nest. Nothing made me feel more cherished than these prayers. The more we pray about our sex lives the better we love each other. So it is a really hard discipline because we have an enemy who doesn't want us to be closer to each other! If I suggest we pray about sex, he never refuses, but when he suggests we pray and offers up thanksgiving to God for what we have together, I'm like a new person. I feel cherished.

What if a husband never gives such a gift as prayer? You know the only answer. You pray. Ask for God's help when things aren't going well. Pray for him before falling asleep at night; pray for him in the morning when you wake up.

Do you know specifically what you want to happen in your sex life? Begin by confessing any bitterness, anger, or worry. Always end with thanks. You could even thank God for your husband's touch right in front of him. He may sense your love in a new way and open up to you more than before.

Here is a composite of many women's prayers for their sex life.

Dear Heavenly Father,

I need your help. Sometimes I feel like a failure as a lover because I don't want to have sex with my husband very often. I selfishly use my lack of libido or tiredness as an excuse. Please give me your perspective! Help me see my husband as worthy of every effort to relate to him sexually. I know all these tips would help us. Give me courage to try a few of these ideas. I know you will bless us for taking time for sex. Help me learn to enjoy him in a whole new way.

In Jesus' Name, Amen

11

A Time to Cherish

Expectations vs. the Power of Taking Responsibility

Proverbs 14:1
"The wisest of women builds her house, but folly
with her own hands tears it down."

I could hardly wait! Our romantic getaway, only three days off, would involve no airport. We'd simply drive to a downtown hotel for two glorious days of relaxation and *hubba hubba*. But I wanted it to be extra romantic. A recent seminar speaker encouraged us wives to tap into our husbands' enjoyment of the visual, so a new outfit for the weekend seemed like a great idea. I even thought of an added twist.

Since we planned to leave on Friday morning, I asked a girlfriend to go lingerie shopping with me on Thursday. We'd find a little something to fit nicely into my husband's top desk drawer. Our outing produced the perfect lacy-but-soft red and white teddy. Now, to get it into his office. *Oh, yeah… 3:00 staff meeting! Great.*

My lookout and I pulled into the parking lot at 3:30, knowing his meeting was already in full swing. Afterward, he'd finish business at his desk and head home, prize

210

in hand. That Dusty Springfield song "Wishing and Hoping" kept playing in my head. I inwardly did a little happy dance and sang, "...*Yeah, just do it, and after you do, you will be hi-i-s.*" My little gift would whet his appetite for our time away together, I just knew it.

Now before you nominate me Wifey of the Year, I have to own up to my more normal self. I rarely concocted such romantic feasts in my love kitchen. I'd been known to stir up a pot of resentment instead. Enjoying my stew alone, I'd live in wishing mode or waiting mode, waiting for him to do something he *should know* I'd like. I *expected* romance to be more like a tennis match where we take turns lobbing the romantic ball back and forth. Often I'd make romantic requests, too.

What about your silent hopes or voiced wishes for romance? In this chapter you'll be challenged to see the difference between three choices:

- Requesting – *Asking him* to do something romantic,
- Waiting – *for him* to do something romantic, and
- Dropping expectations – to *act proactively* for the romance you want.

Our female likes and desires vary greatly, so humor me, please, while I share a few requests that went slightly awry.

My Romantic Request #1 – "Honey, could we have a short 'pillow chat' before we fall asleep?"

The whole idea of going to bed together wasn't for sex. I simply asked for a few wind-down minutes of conversation before sleep. If couples on TV can prop against fluffy pillows and chat in their bed at night, why can't we?

Now you two may *never* retire for the night at the same time, and it may have nothing to do with your sex life. Your internal clocks may just run counter to each other. Some husbands stay up late working, others fall asleep on the couch in front of a screen. Others, like my hubby, head to bed with the wife and doze off five or six seconds after horizontal. Light on or off makes no difference – snoring often regales my nightly beauty ritual. So, what do I do? I quit expecting him to relate to me at bedtime. Instead, I can:

- Remember how hard he's worked today and take note of the mental weight he carries.

- Rejoice that he has no need for sleep aids!

- Realize that when I do crawl into bed, he'll probably snuggle up to me, fulfilling at least part of my need for relating. When he does, if my heart is soft, I'll snuggle back.

- Acknowledge his penchant for falling asleep instantly is in no way meant to rebuff me.

Note: If you are that other wife, the one who regularly retires long before Hubby, you may need encouragement. Do you ever feel lonely as you fall asleep – or do you love that hour of reading a book alone? Have you long since given up thinking of bedtime as relational? Maybe these ideas could serve as a reset button:

- Before heading off to bed, plant a lingering kiss on his lips and tell him you'll see him soon.

- Leave a note on the empty pillow beside you. Tell him you think he's awesome.

- Pray for him to see what he's missing by not joining you for a few minutes, even if he has to get back up to do something.

1. *How* do you feel about going to bed together? What's your bedtime ritual as a couple? _____

_____

_____

_____

My Romantic Request #2 – "Babe, would you take me out dancing for our anniversary?"

In feigned hardness of hearing he answers, "What did you say? Fancy? A fancy dinner for our anniversary? Oh, sure, babe. We'll do that." The rare married guy likes to dance in public, but if you asked him to slow dance naked in the privacy of your bedroom, I bet he'd begrudgingly give in (*Ri-i-ight…*). Social dancing with Hubby may be the most romantic thing in the world, but that doesn't mean it's going to happen. I must talk sense to myself:

- Dancing isn't the ultimate symbol of undying love and affection. The day may come when he'll give me a spin at a wedding, but until then, at such events I will dance with the kids and single ladies.

- My hubby deserves credit for opening doors and jars, kissing me in the kitchen, and laughing at my jokes. Those gestures are romantic, if I choose to see them that way.

- When he takes me out to dinner, I won't allow my thoughts to stray to what he didn't do. I thank him for the fancy dinner.

2. *What does* your husband do that you could consider romantic? _____

_____

_____

_____

My Romantic Request #3 – "Hey, Sweetie, let's cuddle on the couch while we watch TV."

By this time in our marriage, most of us have *our* chair, *our* spot on the sofa. Some of us sit side by side on his-and-her recliners, possibly close enough to hold hands. Remember the days when you used to watch TV? You always sat together, touching.

Awhile back, I decided to make our evenings more relational. I simply began to settle in beside him, no longer kitty-corner on the other couch where we sometimes *played footsie.* I think he liked this position best because it put him at a perfect angle for a foot rub. But I wanted body contact.

After a few weeks of sliding in beside him, out of the blue he turned to me and said, "Honey, I'm hot! You're cooking me! Can't you feel the heat radiating off me?"

Possibly my face prompted his quick disclaimer. "Hey, I don't want to hurt your feelings, Babe… and I love having you here – sometimes – when it isn't so hot…"

I returned to the kitty-corner position, pity party in full swing (no tears, mind you), and choked out an apology for being insensitive. Then, within ten minutes, he asked me to come back and sit beside him. To this day, he regularly pats the seat next to him in an inviting gesture. Go figure.

3. *H*ave you ever made a romantic request which your husband turned down and then later, upon thinking about it, changed his mind? Tell about it. _____

_____

_____

_____

My Romantic Request #4 – "Sweetheart, I'd love a hug or kiss along with your 'I love yous.'"

Those often automatic, sometimes flippant words began to almost irritate me. I wanted sincerity with a *demonstration* of love. Not all the time, just sometimes.

Curious about how other women feel about this, I posted a survey on my blog. Which would you prefer: *more non-sexual touch* or *more words of love*. Since either of these marital staples can run low after a few decades, I asked them which one they received most and which one they wanted more.

You've probably already noticed I'm a touch person, but many women would gladly trade touches for the smallest compliment. Due to men's DNA, non-sexual touching tends to lead from one little touch to the next, to the next, and so on… not necessarily where she wants to go at the moment. *Just a little oxytocin, please.* In this case, the gift of romantic words would be regarded as a heart-stopping sonnet.

The survey results revealed that women of all ages chose what they weren't getting.

4. *W*hich would you choose? More touches or more words of love? Why?

_____

_____

_____

Three Paths to Power

My romantic requests or Expectations didn't move our love life down the path toward Passion; but the other path, Resentment, didn't get us there either. Thankfully, Juli Slattery's book, *Finding the Hero in Your Husband*,[1] helped me get on the right track.

I needed her explanation of the **power** wives have in their homes. The verse from Proverbs 14:1 reminded me that with my own hands I can either build my home or tear it down.

> ***The wisest of women builds her house, but folly***
> ***with her own hands tears it down.***
> **Proverbs 14:1**

We have three paths to the kind of power which builds instead of tears down. As we discuss each one separately, think of them as a three-fold cord like the one referred to in Ecclesiastes 4:12.

- To **drop expectations** and take responsibility for friendship and romance.
- To **forgive our husband** for perceived offenses as well as real ones.
- To **meditate on Truth** to see where real love comes from − God.

Dropping expectations is extremely hard. But we must. Unfulfilled, these troublemakers turn us into victims. An assumption of deprivation keeps happiness just beyond our reach. By hanging on to expectations, someone else holds the job of making us happy. My husband does not want that job, and he's not alone. All husbands wilt under pressure to make a wife happy; they never can.

Author, Linda Dillow's excellent marriage books including *Intimate Issues* and *Creative Counterpart*, span well over three decades. Her most compelling concept, first to her daughters and then to women all over the world, affirms wives' mandate to take responsibility for their own love lives.

If I take more responsibility for the quality of my marriage relationship, things may still not go perfectly. But by walking away from expectations, and prayerfully going after what I want, I'd start to live in the state of **having** what I want.

That thought brings me back to my weekend *getaway story*…

Were you curious what happened when Hubby found his gift in the desk drawer? Did he slip it into his briefcase and race home at almost speeding-ticket pace, more ready than ever for our getaway? Not quite. He left his meeting and went straight to his car without going into his office at all.

215

When I greeted him at the door, he acted upbeat, but completely *normal upbeat*. I pursed my lips together, then puckered, kissed him, and didn't say a word. The item, now heating up his desk, would have to wait patiently for its discovery on Monday.

After our delightful weekend and the sweet harmony of slumber on Sunday night, a slight grin remained on my face all day Monday. When he walked through the door after work, nothing. No special item appeared. *Weird. Is the "gift" in his pocket?* Without waiting another minute, I asked, "Hey, Babe, did you find something in your desk drawer today?"

"Ooooh, about that… well, I did find something. I opened my drawer and, whoa, what is this!? I didn't recognize it, so I thought one of the guys might have put it there as a prank. I took it out to the hall to see who'd own up."

"No… you didn't." By now I'm covering my face with my hands.

"Yup, I did. The guys got a big kick out of it, said they'd *never* think of such a joke. But it sure was a good one, whoever did! Wait…" And here he gave me a squinty-eyed look, "Wait, did *you* do that!?"

True story.

Big question: Besides the good laugh after the fact, did we need the item in the drawer for our weekend? At first look, not at all. However, we both agreed the whole scheme enhanced *my* fun in our getaway. From hatching the plan, to shopping, to sneaking into his office − it all played on my mind during the weekend, and later special times as well. Even though he had no idea what was in his desk, my knowing affected *his* good time. What a domino effect! That's powerful.

5. Consider the following statement: I have a lot of power over the atmosphere in my little realm. Write your thoughts here: _____

_____

_____

_____

I've had to learn the hard way to stop asking my husband to be what I want him to be. What about you? Your husband is not only incapable of *being that guy*, he hates the spoken or unspoken requirement. Most men don't function well under the pressure of our perceived needs. Without realizing it, our silent or spoken demands squelch the desire to give on both sides. When that happens, love begins to fade.

So how do we drop our expectations and get the love we desire? I see two ways, depending on the particulars of your man and your season.

First, if you don't feel emotionally close to him, **work to develop a deeper friendship**. Ask questions about things he loves, speak words of admiration, and show him you like him. If this is a new approach for you, make a commitment to allow time for friendship to build.

I once asked my husband if he liked the idea of being my hero. His response? "Of course! Every man wants to be his wife's hero. That's a no-brainer." Just my clear statement, "You are my hero," impacted my man.

On the other hand, some wives exercise their power to get the love they want through **non-verbal sexual moves**. This is the only way some men can be motivated to engage emotionally. They'd rather not talk, but get right to it. Remember how in early days of marriage, you could engage your man with just a look, a flirt, or a touch? Why not now? Who's changed, you or him? Only you can answer that question.

What are *your* reasons for **not** making a move?

- Marlene says her husband would think her crazy if she made sexual moves.
- Joann says he doesn't give her a chance to entice him because "he's always after me."
- Ida said, "My husband isn't interested in me as a person, just as a sex object."
- Sally admitted she's still angry about age-old issues, so she's not going there.
- Bonnie used to try, but after years of rejection, she's sure he'll turn her down – again.
- Cindy confessed, "No way. Flirting as a married woman is foreign to my nature."

While some of the above statements may seem like excuses, each one is a serious barrier to intimacy. The common thread which hides in all these statements is resentment. Resentment causes wives to completely give up on the romantic part of their relationship. That's where the second path to power comes in: **Forgiveness**.

A Time to Cherish

Oh, how many times I've asked God to fix my hubby when I was the one who needed fixing! I needed to forgive him so I could see the truth about myself. I carried a boatload of resentment over the speck in his eye when I had a log stuck in mine.

> **Why do you see the speck that is in your brother's eye but do not notice the log that is in your own eye? You hypocrite, first take the log out of your own eye, and then you will see clearly to take the speck out of your brother's eye.**
> **Matthew 7:3**

And even when he was wrong, I had to forgive him in order to keep relationship. My resentment would hold our romance hostage until he *saw the need to apologize.* Under those conditions, the sweetness in our relationship would die a slow death. When I refused to forgive, I couldn't see my own sin or my expectations clearly.

You may have to forgive your husband for the same offense over and over again, until you see it through different eyes. Now, I'm not talking about serious breaches of trust. I'm talking about the daily stuff we wish were different. When he doesn't take you on dates, forgets your birthday, comes home late and doesn't ask how your day went. When he rejects your sexual move or acts like 4:00 a.m. is a great time for sex. Jesus told us to forgive our brother "seventy times seven" (Matthew 18:22).

The great power in forgiveness comes when once we reach that point, we can proceed to the part where God tells us to *delight in the Lord and He will give us the desires of our hearts* (Psalm 37:4)! I still recall the day I realized the catch with that verse. His giving depends on the desires of my heart. God will grant the desires of a woman who delights in him.

This discovery helped the verse in Matthew 6:33 make more sense, too. *Seek first the Kingdom of God and his righteousness, and all these things will be added to you.* In the past I kept tripping up on the meaning of *all these things.* What a grand word — *all!* I had to accept that *seeking* the Kingdom of God is a huge prerequisite for receiving *all these things.*

Is God talking to you through these verses? Begin with Proverbs 14:1, then carefully look at Psalm 37:4 and Matthew 6:33. Ask him to reveal the extent of your power in light of forgiving your husband.

6. $\mathcal{D}$ear Lord,_____

_____

_____

_____

Have you given up on the romantic part of your relationship? What do you do when you've tried to forgive, gone for counseling, talked to a friend, and cried out to God? After all that, only one answer remains. We have to remap our brain to think true thoughts, uplifting thoughts, to take "every thought captive" to the obedience of Christ (Romans 12:21).

When we see that Scripture holds the secret to our building power, we're ready to take the third path to power: **meditating on Truth**. As a young girl, I learned an easy trick for doing this. Sometimes this method helped me go to sleep. The idea is to repeat a key phrase over and over, each time emphasizing a different word. For example, my father taught me to repeat the first verse of the 23rd Psalm. *The Lord is my shepherd* by emphasizing a different word each time I repeated the verse: THE Lord is my shepherd. The LORD is my shepherd – and so on. Now, where my marriage is concerned, I can say, I AM grateful for him. I am GRATEFUL for him! I am grateful for HIM. This technique might help you change ingrained, unhealthy attitudes.

Try the method with this verse from Song of Solomon 6:3. *I am my beloved's and my beloved is mine.*

Power also increases as we become aware of our powerlessness over earthly outcomes. How do we give up worrying and watching for results? In reality, there are no predictable outcomes on this side of eternity. Somewhere during midlife, we find that nothing turned out like we anticipated. However, for those in Christ, our ultimate reward, Heaven, is the best one. When we live for the bigger picture, we find strength to move toward our husband with gratefulness. The Bible takes on new meaning and we find joy in meditating.

You and I will always struggle in romance until or unless we give up on it. But should we? Romance keeps a fire going in our soul. God seeks a deep soul-fulfilling romance with us. Should we seek less in our marriages? I am still learning to drop expectations, offer forgiveness, and meditate on Truth.

7. *We* can have the love we desire — by giving it. How will you go after love without any predictions or expectations about how it will turn out? Pray a prayer of submission here. Ask God to help you live in the power you have to build your home. Quote at least one of the above verses in order to pray with more effectiveness. _____

_____

_____

_____

_____

_____

_____

Change Mad to Sad in Conflict

I John 1:6, 7
"If we say we have fellowship with him while we walk in darkness,
we lie and do not practice the truth. But if we walk in the light,
as he is in the light, we have fellowship with one another,
and the blood of Jesus his Son cleanses us from all sin."

When Hubby enters my tiny office for a chat, I usually greet him with a smile and take a break from my computer. On this Tuesday afternoon, however, he found me engaged in a lively phone gab. Engrossed, I barely looked up at him.

Wait. Did he just do that — give me the "time out" sign followed by a cutting motion at his throat? This conversation wasn't at a good stopping point yet, so as my cocked head remained glued to the phone, my eyes returned his glare. Two people clearly crossed each other's line of respect.

To add insult to injury, or insult to irritation to be more exact, the purpose for his rudeness turned out to be trivial — no blood, no flood, no dead cat. I felt disrespected; he felt exactly the same — like a second-rate citizen, not worthy of an ounce of deference.

A Time to Cherish

The chill at dinner confirmed we weren't done here. Not at all. Something else, something much bigger entered the arena. Power Struggle. Combined with its lethal potion, Death to Romance, we were in for another stand-off.

Did I cause this? No way. But, what just happened? I thought back to recent days. Had we made love this week and had I even noticed? Irritations suddenly popped into my mind, revving my ire, and before I knew what hit me, an old panic set in – the paralysing fear that we aren't okay, that this could escalate, if not verbally, certainly mentally.

Here we go again. Like so many times before, when the initial storm passed, we still wouldn't feel close, just in a truce-like limbo. *Why can't we make up like we used to?* And inside, I would die again, becoming a little more numb. *This would bother me if I cared.*

The strangest part of it all was having no real issue to hash out. Unresolved, vague conflict of this kind digs a rut called "Angry Numb." Although some would say we both owed the other a quick apology, we'd long ago learned that this hollow exercise rarely erased the deeper dynamic at play.

No wonder couples check out emotionally. Tired of the fight cycle, they engage less. Anger throws up skewed memories of old wounds as dust thrown into the air blurs vision. No one knows how or why the disconnect came to be. In the confusion, romance dies, joy evaporates, pain piles up, and the sweet friendship life offers in this season evades.

1. *H*ave you experienced a similar disconnect? Describe what it looks like in your house. _____

_____

_____

_____

Alone on my side of the bed that night, I pondered the book I'd been reading about adults who'd been sexually abused as children, *Wounded Heart* by Dr. Dan B. Allender.[2] His explanation of "good girl" pride and self-protective distancing described me well. As I acknowledged my self-righteous anger, the carefully-constructed defense of my withdrawal began to unravel.

To throw my shoulders back and pridefully avoid pain no longer looked godly; it began to look mercenary and energy-sapping. I thought about how angry, fearful tears never got me where I wanted to go. Neither did demanding to be heard. Neither did insisting it all didn't matter.

2. *E*xplain how you distance yourself from relational pain. What made you aware of your resort to this escape? _____

_____

_____

_____

I made up my mind, this time would be different. Dan Allender challenged me to stop backing farther away from intimacy but keep the door open. After work on Wednesday night, he offered to take me out for dinner and I accepted with a forced smile. Though silence ruled the ride to the restaurant, once settled in our booth, I spoke. "Babe, we both felt disrespected, and we still do. Can't it be okay to disagree, for right now, about who disrespected who?"

My statement of equality had never come out quite that calmly before. To defend our own point of view with bristled feathers had always been JOB ONE.

His quiet tension rejected the idea of amicable disagreement; but in that moment I made a decision. I would allow myself to simply be sad. Sad for all the impasses over the years. Sad for incrementally distancing him from my heart. Sad he had done the same. Sad we both dug our heels in to be right. Sad I lived so close to anger.

A kind of softness came with my decision. It felt like a flicker of light. Accepting sadness became my spiritual mandate in order to oust the other default emotions, self-righteous anger and numbness. I let my point sit. In this uncluttered moment in our restaurant booth, I took a deep breath.

I John 1:7 says "But if we walk in the light, as he is in the light, we have fellowship with one another, and the blood of Jesus his Son cleanses us from all sin."

Sadness drove home with us and stayed. We missed the basketball game we both wanted to watch. I took a walk and called a friend, asking her to pray. I rested in the conviction that I must not push for premature resolution or let anger sneak up to build another wall. Not this time.

3. Do you sometimes push for a resolution, thinking it will somehow help? Share a time you did. When did you call a close friend to pray with you?___

_____

_____

_____

My decision to simply be sad changed the way I prayed. It changed the way I looked at this breach-of-respect kind of conflict. When fear couldn't join forces with anger and trap me in its stronghold, kindness entered the picture. And with it came light. The dust settled, and I saw kindness as a brave path instead of a dishonest one.

In the sadness, I was able to distill the fight down to our common struggle – not feeling loved by the other. I grieved for that.

4. Do you and your husband ever doubt the other one's love? What situations make you feel that way? What can you do to draw closer in those times?____

_____

_____

_____

Sadness kept the door of my heart open and soon allowed me to care again. Grief, my silent partner with God, ushered in some needed healing. By late afternoon on Thursday, I felt a slight new warmth toward him. Attraction. Forgiveness. *Why does he look handsome to me?* Friday at breakfast, I smiled. He smiled back.

5. Do you see the danger of allowing numbness to take the place of healthy engagement? How will you allow the light of Christ's love and forgiveness into your conflict through sadness? _____

_____

_____

_____

_____

A Legacy of Cake –
'Til Death Do Us Part

"A great many things can be solved with kindness, even more with laughter,
but there are some things that just require cake."
Leigh Standley

*P*lease, Lord, let this roll call skip us.

Throughout several screenings and finally the biopsy, we'd remained hopeful. But when our urologist spoke the words we least wanted to hear, "Mr. Goforth, you have prostate cancer," we felt as though he'd delivered a one-two knockout punch.

Ever the Optimistic Wife, though, even while we sat across the desk listening to our options, I sucked in a deep breath, set my jaw, and shot an it-will-be-okay look at Hubby. His eyes betrayed even a shred of confidence. He'd been so distraught by my cancer diagnosis so long ago, surely this couldn't be happening. But it was.

Later at home, my bouncy assurances continued. "Radiation's a good choice, Honey." *Maybe not exactly a piece of cake, but certainly not a big deal.* "You'll sail through

225

like I did in my post-chemo radiation." It didn't occur to me that the eleven years since my cancer might have clouded my memory.

Piece of cake? Not quite. Walt's radiation treatments so radically compromised his digestion that within a year he lost more weight than his average-sized frame could safely endure – almost fifty pounds. But with the daily two to three hours blocked off for radiology appointments, a bit of rest, and a few projects, he managed to keep going.

Sleepless nights, constant pain, and a bland diet he likened to damp cardboard made his days almost unbearable. Social events and family functions became nearly impossible. To make matters worse, as his stomach discomfort escalated, so did tension between us. His business-like demeanor limited our conversation to the trivial or mundane, and I refused to accept it. "Look, the least you could do, Babe, is greet me warmly in the kitchen."

The worst was bedtime. I resented the silence when he turned out the light and faced the other side of the room, putting as much distance between us as possible. In the darkness, I felt most rejected. Loneliness seemed to swallow me.

When the loneliness crept into my daytime psyche, it took the shape of anger. I railed against God, but mostly I was angry at the sick one.

Meanwhile, far away in eastern Canada, my sister and her Irish husband dealt with their issues. Throughout the first half of their thirty-some years of marriage, John's sales-management job afforded them a good life – the best restaurants, Carribean travel, and close friendship with a lively group of Irish immigrants who, for decades, met in each others' homes for parties. Though fifteen years older than Patsy, John kept pace with her youthful flair.

Now John was known for loving cake. I can't tell you how many meals in their home ended with Patsy's fabulous cheesecakes, pound cakes, or fluffy coconut cakes. Despite the two thousand miles between us, Patsy and I managed to visit each other for regular, much-cherished *sister fixes*.

One day fairly early in their marriage, Patsy noticed John twisting his wrist oddly as he walked. Tests revealed Parkinson's Disease. She surprised us all by receiving the news with panache. "I will enjoy caring for him. He'll get his cake on a china plate with a silver fork." Those may not have been her words exactly, but they are definitely the jist.

Slowly over the following decade, cake became more of a *project* for John. We'd see him positioned for balance in the corner of the couch, eating his beloved dessert. With each forkful, he'd slump a bit forward, his nose inching closer and closer to the cake. Then, just before he'd start to slip off the couch, someone would notice and, *without removing the plate from his death grip*, help straighten him. We'd laugh, not *at* him, but at his hilarious oblivion to *anything* but the cake.

As Harry Truman said, "There's nothing better than cake than more cake."

Eventually, Patsy fed him, not only cake, but all his food, in public, with no complaint or awkwardness.

When several falls required an ambulance, John's lost mobility, even with a walker, forced Patsy to put him into a nursing home. While fighting despondency, she made his room the classiest one in the building, decorating it with Irish memorabilia and golfing photos. He welcomed guests with a small, well-stocked refrigerator and always some kind of chocolate. He made the nurses laugh every day while my sister went home to an empty bed, a desolate house, and utter aloneness.

Always a busy Type A personality in the past, she learned to slow down and watch TV snuggled into the hospital bed. Years turned to decades as Patsy logged in thousands of hours sitting, talking, laughing, and sometimes weeping with John. As his body weakened, he queried her about their situation. She always directed his attention to a Father who loved them and would see them through.

Her own comforts set aside, Patsy cut John's hair, manicured his nails, and kept up his snappy wardrobe. When she needed a break, John never lacked for a buddy to take him out for coffee and, of course, a piece of cake. His sense of humor and affection kept his friends gladly coming back. The sight of chocolate icing on his chin made them smile. And they loved the Johnisms which never grew old. "How are you feeling, John?" they'd ask.

"With both hands, of course!"

During the final years of John's decline, I flew to Toronto more often. Parkinson's Disease now racked not only his body, but his mind as well. Whether he spoke in clear, lucid conversation or in nonsensical musings, he praised his Patsy. Their mutual devotion impressed all who saw it.

A Time to Cherish

Sometimes, wonderstruck, I would video them together.

Toward the end of one visit, Patsy told John she would take me to the airport the next day. Sitting next to him on the bed, she stroked his cheeks and randomly picked some miniscule piece of flaked skin from his face. I took the phone from my purse and began to video.

"John, when Sandra leaves tomorrow, I'm going to take you out for a nice big, fat, juicy steak, just the two of us. And maybe a movie. What do you think of that?"

In his halting way of half-whispering, he replied, "Oh, I — like that — idea. And I have a — another idea…"

"Oh, what is that, dear?"

"I just won—wondered if when we c-come back, do you th- think we c-could make l-love?"

Just as he finished the phrase "make love," I turned off the video. Not because it didn't seem right to record, but because Patsy and I burst out laughing. We laughed so hard while John looked from me to her. "You — you th- think I'm k-kidding."

Back home, months after my trip, the sacred moment played on my mind — but not enough to improve my attitude toward Walt. I lived in a state of anxiety and fear his disease had somehow convinced him our love life was over. And if so, I wanted to run away. Maybe not permanently, but long enough for him to sting.

I finally made an appointment with a close friend and pastor. In the couple's living room, all the built-up bitterness poured out in hot, desperate tears. "How could he refuse to at least try to relate more intimately? Why is this happening?!" I stopped short of the implied closing words "… to me." *Why is this happening — to me?*

Then my dear friend pulled out the card I least wanted him to play. *The John card.* "Sandi, remember the video you showed us — the one with your sister on the side of John's bed? Remember the tender passion you saw between two lovers who hadn't slept together for almost ten years? *For the entire length of John's disease,* you held a front row seat to real patience, real self-control. You saw sacrificial love in your sister." And here his eyes began to fill with tears of concern for me. "Can you not give Walt a year or so to recover from his illness?"

Oooh. I felt small. And whiny. And self-absorbed. Alone with God later that night, my selfish demands looked very, very ugly. And not new. The insidious vine of discontent had grown tall in my mental yard. Its broad leaves had blocked the vision of my good man, blinding me to all the ways he served me, cared for me, and deeply loved me.

I thought if I could develop even a tiny portion of the patience my sister demonstrated *for over twenty years*, I knew we'd be okay. But God would have to do it, for my strength just wasn't there, so deep was my fear. And he did. Discovering the damage my petulance wreaked in our marriage allowed God to change my heart. I read Proverbs 14:1 with new eyes. I'd been tearing my house down with my own hands! I asked God to make me a wise woman again. In the past I'd been able to build my house, but I'd allowed something important to fall by the wayside. Gratefulness.

A new appreciation began to grow in me. I thanked God for the privilege of sleeping in the same bed with my husband. He showed me how each night is a singular *gift of cake* that could be gone tomorrow. With God's gracious help, I got on the course of encouraging Walt through the *full year* it took him to recover. And recover he did!

On my next trip to Canada, less than a year after the previous one, John couldn't eat regular food anymore. His palate centered completely around cake. In Patsy's apartment, we baked two, a chocolate and a lemon, and froze them in large squares. For the next few days, he smiled when we walked in with cake – just cake. But he ate only a few bites of the first square.

The week after I flew home, Patsy knew his time had come. She asked friends and nursing home staff to allow her and John some alone time. She climbed into his bed and held him in her arms. In God's amazing strength, she found the joy to whisper her love into his ear and tell him it was okay, he could go on ahead to his home.

A Time to Cherish

Do you see each day with the man God gave you as cake? Do you view hardships you overcome in your marriage as a huge part of your legacy? God has equipped you with tools now and hope for the future. We can be sure, the best cake comes on the other side of this journey. I picture John in heaven with a vital new body, maybe even enjoying angel food cake!

> *May the God of hope fill you with all joy and peace in believing,*
> *so that by the power of the Holy Spirit you may abound in hope.*
> **Romans 15:13**

Just One Hour More

Monday morning, sweet repose…
Alarm clock mocks a chilly nose.
You hit the button, defy the world,
"Just one hour more!" our plea's unfurled.
Soft sheet pulled up shuts out the cold,
These early hours are love's pure gold!

Tuesday, fog in frozen air…
Your "G'morning" brushes tousled hair.
Beyond the mist resides the day,
Responsibility is miles away.
Just one hour more in our castle called "Delight,"
Pretending boldly we still have night!

Wednesday, warm in shadows deep…
At not-quite-five we just can't sleep.
In electric darkness hearts beat fast.
Can it be twenty-something years have passed?
With laughing eyes, we seize the hours,
Alarm clock knows — this time is ours!

231

A Time to Cherish

Thursday, billowy clouds drift by.
Your arms surround me, shoulder, thigh.
"No excuse — get up!" sings the sun.
"Work and chores — they must be done!"
But cologne lingers from the night before,
And no one stirs beyond our door…
Your kisses whisper, "Just one hour more…"

Friday dawns all crisp and sweet.
You touch my chin as our eyes meet.
"This love is bliss," you softly say,
"But, Hon, we must get up today.
Alarm went off an hour ago!
Okay, you win, just a minute more — or so…"

Now Saturday's here, a breezy morning.
Your body moves to its symphony of snoring.
From close behind I slide up closer,
Slip a hand over muscular shoulder.
"Honey, today our time is free!
Let's stay 'til noon, or two, or three!"

So thus the years, then decades pass.
While children, grandkids grow up fast.
Time holds no bounds on marital bliss.
The persistent few partake of this.
A thousand glories from heaven pour
Gold, spun from just one hour more.

— Sandra Joan Goforth, 1997

Appendix

AWE Book List

Many of these books have been referenced in the text, and some are included because, as part of my own library, they have helped to form the ideas written here. This list is just a smattering of the wonderful books on the market. We have grouped them loosely for your convenience in choosing what might best meet your needs. Enjoy!

Romance

Love Life For Every Married Couple *by Dr. Ed Wheat*

The Romance Factor *by Alan Loy McGinnis*

Red-Hot Monogamy *by Bill and Pam Farrel*

Kiss Me Like You Mean It *by David Clarke*

Rekindling the Romance *by Dennis Rainey*

Sex Manuals/How-To's

Intended for Pleasure *by Dr. Ed Wheat*

The Gift of Sex *by Dr. Clifford Penner*

Intimate Issues *by Lorraine Pintus and Linda Dillow*

Restoring the Pleasure *by Dr. Clifford Penner*

Sexual Intimacy in Marriage *by Sandra Glahn and W. Cutrer*

The Language of Sex *by Dr. Gary Smalley and Ted Cunningham*

The Act of Marriage Over 40 *by Tim LaHaye*

Psychology/Counseling/Bible Study

The DNA of Relationships *by Dr. Gary Smalley*

Finding the Hero in Your Husband *by Dr. Juli Slattery*

Undefiled *by Harry Schaumburg*

Pulling Back the Shades *by Dr. Juli Slattery*

Boundaries *by Dr. Henry Cloud and Dr. John Townsend*

The Marriage Builder *by Dr. Larry Crabb*

Passion Pursuit: What Kind of Love Are You Making? *by Linda Dillow and Dr. Juli Slattery*

A Woman's Struggle *by Shannon Ethridge*

For Women Only *by Shaunti Feldhahn*

For Men Only *by Shaunti Feldhahn*

Love Your Husband, Love Yourself *by Jennifer Flanders*

Love and Respect *by Emerson Eggerich*

Abuse

Wounded Heart *by Dr. Dan B. Allender*

How to Act Right When Your Spouse Acts Wrong *by Leslie Vernick*

Surprised by the Healer *by Linda Dillow and Dr. Juli Slattery*

Notes

Chapter 2: A Time to Face Reality

1. **Genesis 12:2** – "And I will make of you a great nation, and I will bless you and make your name great, so that you will be a blessing."

    Genesis 22:18 – "And in your offspring shall all the nations of the earth be blessed, because you have obeyed my voice."

2. **Excerpts from Genesis 12: 1-8** – ... So Abram went, as the LORD had told him, and Lot went with him. Abram was seventy-five years old when he departed from Haran. And Abram took Sarai his wife, and Lot his brother's son, and all their possessions that they had gathered, and the people that they had acquired in Haran, and they set out to go to the land of Canaan. When they came to the land of Canaan, Abram passed through the land to the place at Shechem, to the oak of Moreh. At that time the Canaanites were in the land...

3. **Genesis 13:2** – Now Abram was very rich in livestock, in silver, and in gold.

4. **Excerpts from Genesis 12:10-19** – When he was about to enter Egypt, he said to Sarai his wife, "I know that you are a woman beautiful in appearance, and when the Egyptians see you, they will say, 'This is his wife.' Then they will kill me, but they will let you live. Say you are my sister, that it may go well with me because of you, and that my life may be spared for your sake." When Abram entered Egypt,

the Egyptians saw that the woman was very beautiful. And when the princes of Pharaoh saw her... the woman was taken into Pharaoh's house... but the LORD afflicted Pharaoh and his house with great plagues because of Sarai, Abram's wife.

Excerpts from Genesis 20:1-18 – ... And Abraham said of Sarah his wife, "She is my sister." And Abimelech king of Gerar sent and took Sarah. But God came to Abimelech in a dream by night and said to him, ... "the woman whom you have taken, for she is a man's wife."... Then Abimelech called Abraham and said to him, "What have you done to us?"... Abraham said, "I did it because... they will kill me because of my wife..." Then Abraham prayed to God, and God healed Abimelech, and also healed his wife and female slaves so that they bore children. For the LORD had closed all the wombs of the house of Abimelech because of Sarah, Abraham's wife.

5. **Excerpts from Genesis 16:1-6** – Sarai, Abram's wife, took Hagar the Egyptian, her servant, and gave her to Abram her husband as a wife. And he went in to Hagar, and she conceived. And when she saw that she had conceived, she looked with contempt on her mistress.

   Excerpts from Genesis 21:10-12 – So she said to Abraham, "Cast out this slave woman with her son, for the son of this slave woman shall not be heir with my son Isaac."... God said to Abraham, "Be not displeased... Whatever Sarah says to you, do as she tells you, for through Isaac shall your offspring be named."

6. **Excerpts from Genesis 14:11-16** – When Abram heard that his kinsman had been taken captive, he led forth his trained men, born in his house, 318 of them, and went in pursuit as far as Dan. And he divided his forces against them by night, he and his servants, and defeated them and pursued them to Hobah, north of Damascus.

7. **Excerpts from Genesis 18:9-15** – The LORD said, "I will surely return to you about this time next year, and Sarah your wife shall have a son." And Sarah was listening at the tent door behind him. Now Abraham and Sarah were old, advanced in years. The way of women had ceased to be with Sarah. So Sarah laughed to herself, saying, "After I am worn out, and my lord is old, shall I have pleasure?" The LORD said to Abraham, "Why did Sarah laugh and say, 'Shall I indeed bear a child, now that I am old?' Is anything too hard for the LORD?"

8. **Genesis 3:6-7** – So when the woman saw that the tree was good for food, and that it was a delight to the eyes, and that the tree was to be desired to make one wise, she took of its fruit and ate, and she also gave some to her husband who was with her, and he ate. Then the eyes of both were opened, and they knew that they were naked. And they sewed fig leaves together and made themselves loincloths.

9. Wolgemuth, Robert D. and Bobbie. *Couples of the Bible: a One-Year Devotional Study to Draw You Closer to God and Each Other.* Zondervan, 2013, pp. 25–26.

10. **John 3:16** – "For God so loved the world, that he gave his only Son, that whoever believes in him should not perish but have eternal life."

11. **Jeremiah 31:3** – "the LORD appeared to him from far away. I have loved you with an everlasting love; therefore I have continued my faithfulness to you."

12. **John 3:16** – "For God so loved the world, that he gave his only Son, that whoever believes in him should not perish but have eternal life."

    Psalm 36:7 – How precious is your steadfast love, O God! The children of mankind take refuge in the shadow of your wings.

    Psalm 86:5 – For you, O Lord, are good and forgiving, abounding in steadfast love to all who call upon you.

    Romans 5:8 – But God shows his love for us in that while we were still sinners, Christ died for us.

13. Slattery, Julianna. *Finding the Hero in Your Husband: Surrendering the Way God Intended.* Faith Communications, 2004, pp. 45.

Chapter 6: A Time to Choose Your Hormone

1. Dillow, Linda, and Julianna Slattery. *Passion Pursuit: What Kind of Love Are You Making?* Moody Publishers, 2013.

2. Schaumburg, Harry. *Undefiled, Redemption from Sexual Sin.* Moody Publishers, 2009.

3. LaHaye, Tim, et al. *The Act of Marriage after 40: Making Love for Life.* Zondervan Pub. House, 2000.

4. Clarke, David. *Kiss Me Like You Mean It.* Revell, 2009, pp. 117.

5. LaHaye, Tim, et al. *The Act of Marriage after 40: Making Love for Life.* Zondervan Pub. House, 2000.

Chapter 7: A Time to Help Your Man

1. Roberts, Ted. "The Battle Plan For Purity." *Conquer Series*, Kingdomworks Studios, 2019, www.conquerseries.com/.

2. "Screen Accountability™." *Covenant Eyes*, Covenant Eyes, 2019, www.covenanteyes.com/.

Chapter 9: A Time to Negotiate

1. Lawton, Shailer Upton, and Jules Archer. *Sex without Fear.* Sex Guidance Publications, 1951.

2. Schaumburg, Harry. *Undefiled, Redemption from Sexual Sin.* Moody Publishers, 2009.

3. **Excerpts from Psalm 139** – O Lord, you have searched me and known me… for you formed my inward parts; you knitted me together in my mother's womb… my frame was not hidden from you, when I was being made in secret, intricately woven in the depths of the earth. Your eyes saw my unformed substance…

4. **Romans 12:1** – I appeal to you therefore, brothers, by the mercies of God, to present your bodies as a living sacrifice, holy and acceptable to God, which is your spiritual worship.

    1 Peter 3:1 – Likewise, wives, be subject to your own husbands, so that even if some do not obey the word, they may be won without a word by the conduct of their wives,

5. **1 Corinthians 6:19** – Or do you not know that your body is a temple of the Holy Spirit within you, whom you have from God? You are not your own, for you were bought with a price. So glorify God in your body.

6. Chapman, Gary. *The Five Love Languages*. Northfield Publishing, 2004.

Chapter 10: A Time to Practice, Practice, Practice

1. **Romans 12:1-2** – I appeal to you therefore, brothers, by the mercies of God, to present your bodies as a living sacrifice, holy and acceptable to God, which is your spiritual worship. Do not be conformed to this world, but be transformed by the renewal of your mind, that by testing you may discern what is the will of God, what is good and acceptable and perfect.

2. Penner, Clifford, and Joyce Penner. *Restoring the Pleasure: Complete Step-by-Step Programs to Help Couples Overcome the Most Common Sexual Barriers*. W Publishing Group, an Imprint of Thomas Nelson, 2016.

3. Gregoire, Sheila Wray. *31 Days to Great Sex: Love. Friendship. Fun*. Word Alive Press, 2014.

4. Farrel, Bill, and Pam Farrel. *Red-Hot Monogamy*. Harvest House Publishers, 2006.

5. Penner, Clifford, and Joyce Penner. *The Married Guy's Guide to Great Sex: Building a Passionate, Intimate, and Fun Love Life*. Tyndale House Publishers, Inc., 2017, pp. 53–54.

6. Penner, Clifford, and Joyce Penner. *Restoring the Pleasure: Complete Step-by-Step Programs to Help Couples Overcome the Most Common Sexual Barriers*. W Publishing Group, an Imprint of Thomas Nelson, 2016.

Chapter 11: A Time to Cherish

1. Slattery, Julianna. *Finding the Hero in Your Husband: Surrendering the Way God Intended.* Faith Communications, 2004, pp 32-33.

2. Allender, Dan B. *The Wounded Heart.* NavPress, 1995.

Acknowledgements

If you've ever jumped into a cool lake not realizing how much colder the water was than you realized, you might have an idea how I felt as we began to teach classes from the original *A Time to Embrace* – both exhilarated and surprised. Though exhilarated to see binders give way to a hold-in-your-hand book, we soon realized the need for a revision which would reorder the chapters, clarify points in each chapter, and tighten up the material for better use by small groups.

Now, after over a year of working and reworking the manuscript, through much collaboration, the project has reached completion. Karen Holmes, Sheri Hunt, Candee Brandau, and Kim Coburn brought fresh insight to the changes and worked on organizing as well as editing. Thank you, ladies, for your gift of attention to detail! Thanks also to my talented young neighbor, Jeanette Rath, who while honeymooning, typed and organized the notations. How can I ever thank Julia Anne Tepera for her expert proofreading!

Hill Country Christian Writers also cheered me onward. Karen Sheppard, Judy Watters, and Elizabeth Pavlov kept the project in their prayers. And speaking of prayers, we all relied on our AWE Prayer Team to hold us up through classes as well as the revision process. Alma Wakefield, Twyla Tenney, Beryl Hartwig, and Linda Rowe, thank you for caring enough to pray specifically and fervently.

The encouragement and inspiration of our AWE Leadership Team constantly reminded me of the changed marriages resulting from our classes. Thank you Gwen Cunningham, Leatine Fasano, Jennie Hewlett, Margarita Rivera, Chris Hansen, Betty Hicks, Candee Brandau, and Kelly McMahan for not only keeping up your gentle pressure to finish, but also offering help with edits.

Then there's my husband, who approved this message. Oh how many nights, confident of his sound sleep, I crept out of bed to spruce up a chapter which often included a story about him. What a brave soul to be the willing subject of such exposure! Thank you, Babe.

AWE Confidentiality Statement

I acknowledge that a study surrounding issues of marriage, aging, and sexuality may necessarily involve sensitive sharing. Such sharing will not leave this room. We agree this is a place of kindness, prayer, and non-judgment. We will listen with compassion and never mention each other's tender topics to our family or anyone but our Heavenly Father. This kind of care makes our study safe.

Disclaimer Regarding Scope of AWE

This class is not for counseling purposes nor can we refer. We are here to grow in the understanding of God's design for marriage. Though most marriages suffer some level of sadness and disconnection at various times and seasons, if you have any ongoing abuse or addiction in your home, we suggest you seek professional counsel immediately.

I affirm both above statements.

_____   Date: _____